DEDICATED TO THOSE
WHO WANT **MORE** OUT OF LIFE AND TO THOSE WHO WANT
THEIR LIVES **TO COUNT**
BEFORE THE **ONE WHO REALLY MATTERS.**

ABOUT THE AUTHOR

Tara Furman is the founder and CEO of Knowing God Ministries, a 501(c)3 tax exempt non-profit ministry established in 2010. She grew up in Cary, North Carolina, where she married her high school sweetheart, Tim, whom she met in junior high school! Tim and Tara live with their children Will (12) and Caroline (10), not to mention Jake, their yellow Lab (who should have been named Marley!).

Tara has written and self-published several books:

A Prayer Journal, Intimacy with God: Your Daily Guide to Prayer

Two Seven-Week Bible Studies: Intimacy with God and Created for Purpose

A Christmas Keepsake Journal

In 2007, Tara started a speaking ministry that has grown from local to regional to national in scope. In 2011, Tara began a statewide Women's Discipleship luncheon called Iron Sharpens Iron. She manages a volunteer staff of 7 and a Board of Directors of 8. On her website, www.knowinggodministries.net ,she offers resources vital for a woman's spiritual growth, and a devotional blog that suggests practical ways to know God personally in everyday life.

Tara's favorite things include spending time with her extended family and close friends. She loves to eat her husband's amazing, creative cooking, because he is a "grill master. " She also enjoys her kids' sporting activities. On any given day, you can find Tara in the carpool line at their school, feverishly wrapping up part one of her "workday" and mentally preparing for part two of that day while she savors her "priority blessings," Tim, Will and Caroline.

To invite Tara to speak to your group, go to www.knowinggodministries.net

Contents

Week 1 | Your Life was Created For a Purpose 1

    Day 1 | You Were Created for a Purpose 3

    Day 2 | Your Life is Not a Coincidence 9

    Day 3 | Your Life has a Good Plan 15

    Day 4 | Your Life is Not a Scarlet Letter 19

    Day 5 | Review. 23

Week 2 | Misled by a World and Religious System . . . 25

    Day 1 | Where Am I Going? 27

    Day 2 | Have I Been Brainwashed? 31

    Day 3 | Switching Paths. 35

    Day 4 | Sister Super Christian 39

    Day 5 | Review. 45

Week 3 | The Church Girl and the Jesus Girl. 47

    Day 1 | The Church Girl and the Jesus Girl 49

    Day 2 | Church Girl? Jesus Girl? 53

    Day 3 | The Jesus Girl 57

    Day 4 | Church Girl to Jesus Girl. 61

    Day 5 | Review. 65

Week 4 | Shifts of the Heart 67

    Day 1 | A Paradigm Shift in the Heart 69

    Day 2 | Waking our Hearts. 73

    Day 3 | The Secret Places of the Heart 77

    Day 4 | The Secret Attitudes of the Heart 81

    Day 5 | Review. 87

Week 5 | Listening for Purpose 89

    Day 1 | You Were Created to Hear from God 91

    Day 2 | The Soil of our Heart. 95

    Day 3 | Hearing From God Personally 99

    Day 4 | How to Hear His Voice 105

    Day 5 | Review. 111

Week 6 | Obedience is Key 113

    Day 1 | Our Lineage. 115

    Day 2 | Lifestyle Changes 119

    Day 3 | The Power of Living Obediently. 123

    Day 4 | Baby Steps. 127

    Day 5 | Review. 133

Week 7 | Finishing the Race 135

    Day 1 | Your Talents and Abilities 137

    Day 2 | Taking the "Jesus Thing" Too Far 143

    Day 3 | Dream Again 149

    Day 4 | Run so as to Win the Prize 155

    Day 5 | Review. 159

INTRODUCTION

Have you ever said to yourself, *"There's got to be more to life than this?"* Have you ever wondered what God's purpose is for your life, or if God even has a purpose for your life?

Cover to cover, the Bible reveals that God uses very ordinary people to accomplish extraordinary tasks. Their résumés by today's standards would probably never have qualified them for jobs of great significance. In fact, the people God used in Bible times were very average people.

- A man named Noah built a boat and preserved the entire human race.

- A man named Abraham believed God, and provided the model for sacrifices and ceremonies that pictured for the world God's terms for man to have a right relationship with Him. Abraham's descendants would also record God's revelation to man in what we call the Bible.

- A dreamer named Joseph preserved the remnant of Israel when a famine threatened the people with annihilation.

- An idolatrous Moabite woman named Ruth became the great grandmother to David, one of the most successful kings prior to Christ's birth.

- A young shepherd boy named David would became one of Israel's greatest kings.

- A teenage girl named Mary became the mother of Jesus.

- Unschooled, ordinary men like Peter and John forever changed the world as we know it.

- A murderer named Paul became one of the most successful missionaries the world has ever known.

I'm merely scratching the surface here. But one thing all of these people had all had in common: they walked with the God of the Universe each day. They were not perfect, but they were plugged in to the God of the Universe so that they could know what He wanted them to do in order to live lives that were purposeful.

The God of the Bible is the same God today. There's more to life than mere existence and going through the motions each day. Wherever you may live, in whatever corner of the world you may *"do life,"* God has a specific purpose and a particular plan for YOU! Despite your past, your present circumstances, or your *"stuff,"* God did not create you to muddle through each week, month, and year in mundane living. And He did not intend for you to content yourself with pew-sitting mediocrity once a week, either. Instead, the God of the Universe has destined each one of us to live a life that counts, a life of significance and meaning.

Finish the Race

A life of purpose will not require a fancy degree from a prestigious university. It will not require a ton of money for an initial investment. But make no mistake, finding and living our God-ordained purpose in each season of our life will require hard work, determination, resolve, and wholehearted commitment. But, dear sister, know deep within your being that there's a thrill and an excitement you can only have when you are engaging in what you are created you to do. Nothing this world has to offer can substitute for that. In fact, the peace, joy and contentment that come from living in God's purpose for us cannot be described or even articulated adequately.

There will be days when you may want to quit. Maintaining purpose will require swimming upstream in a downstream world – not just for a week or a month or a season or for the duration of this study – but as a lifestyle. This study is intended to bring shifts in thinking; shifts in priorities and in our perspective on life. There will be times you will want to put the study down because it requires you to address issues or circumstances that have long been swept under the rug. But don't do that, or you may miss out on all God has for you.

God never deals with us or leads us to make changes to give us boring, restricted lives. He wants to lead us to freedom, purpose, meaning and significance, and ultimately on a journey of lifetime that will forever impact our corner of the world and the generations to come!

Suggestions for Study

This is a lifestyle study. Accordingly, you should go through it slowly and methodically. Allow the passages of Scripture to become a part of the fabric of your being. If you are taking this in a small group setting, you may want to consider breaking up the weeks to go through 1 week in 2.

The Prayer Journal, *Intimacy with God: Your Daily Guide to Prayer* is suggested for use with this study. Whatever day of the week you may be working on this study, turn to that page. Write the date. Record any points from the day's study that you desire to remember or review. If God blows you away with revelation that He desires you live out each day, turn to your *"Listening"* Section. Write the date on the left side and what God has said on the right side. Writing it down helps us to remember and makes it more likely for us to follow through with real obedience to what we've studied.

Review each day

When we close the cover of our study each day without allowing the Lord to solidify what we've learned and what He wants us to apply, we miss out on hearing how He wants us to respond. Take time each day to review what you've underlined and to review the passages of Scripture that were meaningful. Quite often, this is God speaking to you. Don't miss what He wants to say and how He wants you to apply what you've learned.

Review at the end of the week

The goal of this study is to bring about a lifestyle shift and a shift in thinking. It's important for the material to become a part of your everyday thinking. Take time to review what you've learned each week. This will be the key to understanding how God wants you to respond to what you've studied. It's your willingness to respond to these promptings that opens the door for a purposeful life.

PREDOMINATE BIBLE USED: New International Version (NIV)

1

Your Life was Created For a **Purpose**

WEEK ONE

Day 1 | You Were Created for a Purpose

Day 2 | Your Life is Not a Coincidence

Day 3 | Your Life Has a Good Plan

Day 4 | Your Life is NOT a Scarlet Letter

Day 5 | Review

CREATED FOR PURPOSE

WEEK 1 | DAY 1

TODAY'S TREASURE
...
"THIS IS TO MY FATHER'S GLORY,
THAT YOU BEAR MUCH FRUIT..."
JOHN 15:8

YOU WERE CREATED FOR A PURPOSE

The God Who sits enthroned above the circle of the earth[1] –
    Who created the starry hosts...[2]
        Who calls them by name...[3]
            Who does GREAT things beyond our understanding...[4]
                Who made the sand a boundary for the sea, an everlasting barrier it **cannot cross...**[5]
                    The ONE **Who spoke** the Universe into existence...[6]

Is God Most High!
    He is the Ancient of Days.
        He is the One Who created the seasons.[7]
            He is the Self-Sustaining One and answers to no one![8]
        He is the Beginning and End; the Alpha and the Omega; the First and the Last.[9]
            He is the One Whom every human being will stand before one day.[10]
            He is the God of Abraham, Isaac, and Jacob.

The God of Moses, Joshua, Deborah, Job, Esther, Ruth, Samuel, David, Mary, Peter and Paul.

This same God who created the heavens, the Earth, the sea and everything in it, is also the God who engages His creation in concrete, definitive and personal ways.

Since 2003, I have come to know this God – not from afar, but up close and personally. Although I became a child of God in 1980, it's only been in the last 10 years that I've **really** *come to know Him personally.*

---

1   Isaiah 40:22
2   Isaiah 40:26
3   Isaiah 40:26
4   Job 26:36
5   Job 38:10-11
6   Psalm 33:6-9
7   Genesis 1:14
8   Romans 11:33-36
9   Revelation 22:13
10   Revelation 20

CREATED FOR PURPOSE

The relationship I have with the God of the universe did not come from sitting on a pew on Sunday mornings.[11] Nor did this relationship come from attending Bible study each week. This relationship did not happen by serving relentlessly at church functions.[12]

I found the God of the Universe when all alone … Catapulted into faith by painful, dark seasons – when all I had were my tears, a shard of faith, a Bible and God Himself.

So on those dark days, instead of running to the phone or email or to *People* magazine or busying myself with something to take my mind off of my circumstances[13], I ran to the Bible … Hoping and praying that this collection of sacred books from antiquity would:

>Provide the answers and solutions I so desperately needed.
>>Help me to find the God I was raised to know...
>>>Provide hope on days that seemed hopeless…

And you know what happened? Miracle upon miracle: in those hard places, at every turn, in every need and with every worry, ANSWERS CAME! Not just any answers, either. Answers came that gave concrete, definitive guidance and peace. And it wasn't just circumstantial peace that's fleeting because it's based upon your situation; it was peace deep within the core of my being. Often my circumstances stayed the same, **but I was different.**

Why?

Because I met the God of the Bible. And dear sister, He is real! He's not just a *"Sunday morning God"* – He is real and personal. God is a knowable and approachable God. Just as Moses encountered God in a burning bush[14] in the desert, I encountered God in a chair in my living room.

There were many days when it seemed as if the words on the pages of this old, old book had been written specifically with my pain and circumstances in mind. I've learned that this is one of the awesome things about God. He speaks in plain language right off the pages of Scripture. It is one of the most mind-blowing things to me that the God of the universe is willing to speak intimately, personally and practically to me and whoever else is willing to truly seek Him.

During this painful season, it was if something inside of me clicked. For the first time in my adult life, despite my past and despite my lukewarm, mediocre faith, I realized that God is a very real Person, who knows and loves me intimately. And in the midst of some very hard circumstances, I learned that **Jesus works** and that He has and continues to have a good plan and purpose for my life.

In the last 10 years, as I've learned to walk with God on a daily basis, starting in very ugly, grim circumstances, He has taken the bad and used it for good by allowing me to impact my corner of the world in profound

---

11   Please hear my heart, I'm not advocating NOT going to church.
12   It was in these places that the desire grew from within to know Him personally for myself. Not through someone else's relationship with Him.
13   We didn't have facebook back then or I would have been on facebook.
14   Exodus 3:4

WEEK 1 | DAY 1

ways. The things I will share in this Bible study have come firsthand from the overflow of my relationship with Him. He has empowered this very simple, ordinary woman to:

- Self-publish a homemade Prayer Journal that helps women grow in prayer and organize their prayer lives.

- Self-publish a Bible Study that has transformed hearts, lives and marriages by helping women to know the God of the Universe.

- Self-publish a Christmas Journal that helps people keep and celebrate the TRUE meaning of Christmas .

- Start a non-profit Women's Ministry called *Knowing God Ministries*, whose mission is to help women KNOW God personally – not just know *about* Him.

- Begin a statewide Women's Discipleship luncheon called *Iron Sharpens Iron*.

- Start a speaking ministry that has grown from regional to statewide to national opportunities.

- Manage a volunteer staff of 7.

- Manage a Board of Directors of 8.

I've done those things while being a wife, a mom, and a *"Chief Home Officer."* Please know that I am very ordinary. I did not score well on the SAT; I had to work very hard to maintain a *"B"* average in school. In fact, apart from God, I tend to be insecure and introverted.

The reason I share this with you is not to boast or brag, but to encourage you that **God has a specific purpose and plan for everyone He has created.** Not just for me, but for you too! Regardless of your past; regardless of your present circumstances – God has a plan for your life! And it is a good plan. It is His desire that all of us impact our corner of the world in a meaningful, significant way.

However, I would have never known this, had I not met Him personally and intimately, and begun following Him intentionally. This will be the key to living purposefully.

GOD WANTS TO USE YOU

1. **Read 1 Corinthians 1:26-29. Who does God delight in using?**

   _____ (v27)

   _____ (v27)

   _____ (v28)

   _____ (v29)

   _____ (v29)

2. **Why does He choose people like this? (v29-30)** _____

3. **So if we boast, who are we to boast in? (v31)** _____

CREATED FOR PURPOSE

Please do not be insulted or think that I'm calling you weak, foolish, or lowly! I am not. However, many people[15] do not think that they could ever be used for anything special or of significance. We tend to think that God only uses *"perfect special people,"* people without baggage or without a past. Not average, ordinary people.

But according to Scripture, God delights in using *the weak, the foolish, the lowly, and the despised*. He does not necessarily call the people who are wise by human standards or those who are influential or of noble birth. He has no favorites.

4. **Read Luke 2: 8-11. To whom did God first announce the birth of His Son, Jesus?**

   _____

Please note, God did not announce **the most important event in world history** to kings or to the influential or those of noble birth. He gave the announcement of all announcements to shepherds. Shepherds were men without homes, with dirty clothes and dirt under their fingernails, living in fields, tending sheep.

GOD'S DESIRE FOR EACH OF US

5. **What is God's desire for each of us?**

   a. John 1:12 _____

   b. John 15:8 _____

   c. What amount of fruit? _____

6. **What do you think it means to** *"bear much fruit?"*

   _____

   _____

Sweet sister, the God of the universe has ordained that your precious life bear fruit. And not just a little fruit, ***but much fruit.***

Fruit bearing has nothing to do with grapes, apples and oranges. In other words, God has not appointed you to a mediocre, mundane life where you just muddle through and then die. Your life has been set apart for significance. God wants your life to count for all eternity. He wants your life to matter.

Noble Perry writes in his book, *Unleashed*[16], *"God has called each one of us to embrace life, not merely to endure it. He wants us to have overwhelming victory[17], to conquer sin and death[18], to not get tired of doing the right thing[19], and to make a difference rather than make excuses[20]."*

---

15 I used to think this way too
16 *Unleashed,* Noble Perry, Tyndale House Publishers 2012, p4
17 Romans 8:37
18 1 Corinthians 15:57
19 Galatians 6:9
20 Acts 22:16

WEEK 1 | DAY 1

"Bearing much fruit" is not just for the preachers and teachers and heroes of the world. **It's attainable for ALL of us.** It's what we were created for… it's our purpose for being on planet earth. I'm sick of the enemy's scheme of convincing believers that only a few lives in each generation are truly significant. This simply isn't true. This contradicts what God's Word says and is lie from the pit of hell.

"Bearing much fruit" will look differently for all of us. Just as no two fingerprints are alike, no two lives that bear fruit will look the same. We have to be careful of comparisons. But in different lives, bearing significant fruit will do the same thing.

7. What do all fruit-bearing lives do? _____

Though each one of us will bear fruit that looks differently from the other, God's primary concern is that He be glorified. God is glorified most when people come to know Him personally and worship Him anew; when lives are restored and healed and bear witness to the fact of His Presence at work in homes, communities, schools, places of business, friendships, and churches.[21] This, my friend, is a significant, fruitful life. We'll go into greater detail about what that means as the study progresses.

God does not create mind-numb robots. He gives us the gift of free will to make choices for ourselves. He will never interfere with our free will. He allows us to live our lives as we please. *It's up to us if we desire to live fruit-bearing, purposeful lives.* In fact, to live a life that bears fruit in this day and age will not happen automatically. **You will have to be intentional about doing that.**

JOURNAL RESPONSE

Take a few moments to meditate on our study today.

Were there particular Scripture(s) or statement(s) that spoke to you personally?

1.

2.

2.

---

21 We'll go into much greater depth in future weeks.

CREATED FOR PURPOSE

WEEK 1 | DAY 2

TODAY'S TREASURE
...
"YOU WILL ALL SEE HEAVEN OPEN AND THE ANGELS OF GOD GOING UP AND DOWN ON THE SON OF MAN, THE ONE WHO IS THE STAIRWAY BETWEEN HEAVEN AND EARTH.
JOHN 1:51 NLT

YOUR LIFE IS NOT A COINCIDENCE

Since the beginning of time, every human being – regardless of economic, ethnic, or cultural background – was created to KNOW his or her Creator, the Living God of the Universe. We were not created to know Him through another person's relationship; to just know Him academically, or from afar, or even through a religious experience. We were created to KNOW HIM in a vibrant personal relationship.

1. In whose image are we made? (Genesis 1:27) _____

2. Whom does God accept? (Acts 10:34-35) _____

3. Exodus 34:14 NLT, *"God is passionate about His relationship with you."*

    What are God's feelings about being in relationship with us? _____
    _____

4. Ephesians 3:12 NLT, *"Because of Christ and our faith in Him, we can now come fearlessly into God's presence assured of His glad welcome."*

    a. How can those who belong to Christ come into God's presence?
    _____

    b. What is God's response? _____

As human beings, we are made in the image of the God of the universe. This same God does not show favoritism, but accepts people from every nation. And He is passionate about being in relationship with those who fear Him and do what is right. He loves us so much that He sent His only Son, Jesus, to Earth, so that all who receive and believe Him, can become children of the Most High God. When we become His child by faith, the Bible says we can FEARLESSLY come into God's presence *assured* that He's glad to see us.

CREATED FOR PURPOSE

STEP ONE: KNOW GOD PERSONALLY

The year was 1980. I was in the car with my neighbor's mom as she took us home from school. Most every day, she talked about Jesus, the way to God's heaven. She described sin as being the wrong things we do – such as disobeying or talking back to my parents or lying or cheating in school or fighting with my sister. I became very aware of the fact that I was guilty of this thing she called sin.

It was on one of those many trips home from school that ***I made the deliberate decision*** to ask Jesus into my life. I can still remember where I was as we rode down the city street when I prayed that one simple prayer. I didn't understand everything about God, but I did understand three vitally important things:

1. I was a sinner and needed a way of being made right with God.

2. In order to be made right with God, I had to believe that Jesus is God's Son.

3. I had to personally receive Jesus into my life.

FINDING HIM PERSONALLY

5. **Read John 1:12 again. Who is the *"Him"* referred to in these verses?** _____

6. **What are the two qualifiers to being a child of God?**

    4. _____

    5. _____

How easy to sit in church and think, *"I'm a child of God."* Yet, the Bible is CLEAR on how we become children of God. And sadly, it contradicts what I hear through the media and sometimes through ministers, pastors, and priests who have said, *"We are all God's children."* The Bible says we are ALL God's creation, but we are not all *God's children*. Becoming a child of God is personal choice. This is the first step to bearing fruit.

7. **This is a contradiction of what many of us have heard and known all our lives. Is it to you? Share your thoughts.**

    _____

    _____

I don't want you to assume that just because you are in this Bible study, or go to church each Sunday, or live a moral life, or have been baptized, that Jesus resides in your life. I've encountered many people who have assumed they are *"Christians"* because:

- Theoretically, we live in a Christian country.
- They attend church regularly.
- They've joined a church.
- They've been baptized.

WEEK 1 | DAY 2

- They live by the Golden Rule.
- Their mother or grandmother are strong believers.
- They've read the Bible.
- They're not Jewish or Muslim or Buddhist.
- They *believe* in God.

Believing in God is NOT ENOUGH. The Bible says that even the demons believe.[22] Belief in Jesus, God's Son and His way of being made right with Him is the ONLY way to God's heaven. The Bible says:

John 14:6, Jesus answered, *"I am the way and the truth and the life. No one comes to the Father except through Me."* (Notice He says He is THE way, not A way.)

Acts 4:12, speaking of Jesus, *"Salvation is found in no one else, for there is no other name under heaven given to men by which we must be saved."*

8. How does Today's Treasure Verse describe Jesus, the Son of Man?

_____

Jesus is the stairway between heaven and earth. Jesus is the Way to the Father. There is no other name given to men by which we can be saved. The first step to living a life of purpose and an eternally significant life on earth is making sure you are a child of God!

If you cannot remember when you made the deliberate decision to believe and receive Christ, there may be a good chance that He's not there! Jesus is a gentleman. He does not push His way into our lives. Accepting God's way to heaven is an individual choice.

9. Can you remember when you made the deliberate decision to open the door of your heart to believe and receive Jesus? Would you be willing to share?

_____

JUST TO BE SURE

Just in case you are not sure or perhaps you've forgotten… Or perhaps you were brought up in a religion that it was decided for you and are just not sure… Let's be sure together! It's really simple. With believing faith, bow your head now and tell God:

1. "I have done wrong things (called sin) and I want to turn, with Your help, Lord, from sin.

2. I believe Jesus is God's Son and way of being right with God.[23]

3. I invite You now to come into my life." Amen.

You may not understand everything you'd like to understand about the Bible, Jesus or God. But that does not matter in God's eyes! If you have prayed this prayer with simple faith, you have just completed the first step of living the life and receiving ALL God desires to give you! Your eternal destiny has changed![24] Rejoice!

---
22 James 2:19
23 John 14:6, "I am the way, the truth and the life. No one comes to the Father except through Me."
24 If you have any questions about becoming a child of God, please see your Bible study leader, your pastor or minister or feel free to con-

CREATED FOR PURPOSE

Share this with someone, perhaps your Bible study leader or your friend if you prayed this today. I don't mean to sound morbid, but if you were to die today, you can confidently know that you would go to heaven. It's not a matter of, *"I hope I'll go to heaven when I die."* It's now a certainty. Please note, it is vital that you complete step one. If not, the rest of the study will be irrelevant and will not make sense to you.

STEP TWO: TAKE ADVANTAGE OF YOUR CIRCUMSTANCES

Read Acts 17:24-31

10. According to verse 26, what does God do? _____

11. What is His motive for doing this? _____

12. Is He far away? _____

13. What is His desire for each one of us? (verse 28) _____

> According to Scripture, God Divinely places us:
> In this century,
> In this generation and
> In the various places in the world in which we live…

So that ***we will seek Him and perhaps reach out for Him and find Him.*** You and I were placed on planet Earth strategically during this time period. Why? Because God knew that we might reach out for Him and find Him. Life is not a coincidence. Where you live; where you work; who your friends and your family are – all of that is NOT a coincidence. It has been set in motion by the God of the universe that we might live and move and have our being in Him.

14. What does to *"live and move and have our being in Him,"* (Acts 17:28) mean to you?

_____

Though we think God is far away, because He is invisible – He is not far. He is near and close, desiring that each one of us would live and move and have our being in Him. **We will spend the rest of the study developing this concept.** For *"living and moving and having our being in Jesus"* is what we were created for. God has a plan for your life. It is particular and specific in the location He has you.

nect with the *Knowing God Ministries* website.

WEEK 1 | DAY 2

JOURNAL RESPONSE

Take a few moments to meditate on our study today.

Were there particular Scripture(s) or statement(s) that spoke to you personally?

1.

2.

3.

CREATED FOR PURPOSE

WEEK 1 | DAY 3

TODAY'S TREASURE
...
"FOR I HAVE COME THAT THEY
MAY HAVE LIFE AND HAVE
IT TO THE ABUNDANCE."
John 10:10

Your Life has a Good Plan

Ten years ago, if you would have told me what I'd be doing at this point in time with my life, I would have told you that you were absolutely nuts. Crazy! Why? Because the older I get, the more introverted I become.

Decision making? I tend to be indecisive. Making up my mind is something I struggle with.
    Leadership? I'd rather follow. It's safer that way – no one is judging you or criticizing you when you're not the one making the decisions.
        Writing? When I first sensed God calling me to write, I wanted to run from it.
            Speaking? Yes, I majored in speech communications in college, but the kind of speaking I do now is NOT what I studied in college.[25]

So you see, I NEVER, EVER, EVER would I have imagined this. *NOR would I have chosen this for myself.*[26]

But can I tell you that I love my life! And every day that I say "YES" to God, I have a peace deep within the core of my being that I've never had before. There's a quiet assurance and conviction that I am exactly where God wants me, doing exactly what God wants me to be doing.

Yet, please know, this does not mean that my life is perfect or problem-free – it's not! This also does not mean that I have a life of health, wealth and prosperity. Faith has required me to step out of my comfort zone and (if you'll pardon the mixed metaphor) swim upstream in a downstream world.

What's more, since starting this journey 10 years ago, I've dealt with my daughter's diagnosis of a very serious chronic disease, a fluke birth defect in my son that nearly took his life at the age of 10, great personal loss and pain, and a tsunami of epic proportions that makes it nothing short of a miracle that I have an intact, solid marriage. Along with this great tsunami, a degree of insecurity came along that made me wonder if I'd ever recover or be the same. At one time, I even despaired of life.

But without hesitation, I can tell you that ANY woman who says yes to God can experience a deep-down satisfaction that can only come from God Himself. She will live life like few others in her corner of the world. She will have a life of great purpose, a life that matters for all eternity.

A GOOD PLAN FOR ME?

1. **Read John 10:10. Fill in the blanks.**

---

25   In fact, before my ministry partner started traveling with me and praying for me – I'd almost be physically sick before walking on a stage.
26   More on this later too!

CREATED FOR PURPOSE

"For I have come that they may have _____ and have it to the _____."

Whose words are these? _____

I love the way the Amplified Bible phrases it, *"I [Jesus] came that they may have and enjoy life, and have it in abundance (to the full, till it overflows)."*[27]

Please know that when I talk about enjoying life, I'm not talking about swinging from the chandelier. And I'm not necessarily talking about financial wealth. I'm referring to the deep-down peace and joy we can have in life through our relationship with Jesus despite our circumstances. This also doesn't mean that we do not get frustrated, upset or irritated – but it means that we can be at peace and have joy even when life is not necessarily fun. Abundant living is experiencing the presence and the power of God in our everyday lives.

God did not create us to have a miserable, humdrum life. He did, however, create us to work hard and to find and operate in the gifts and the callings that He has placed upon our lives. This is how we begin living in the abundance.

2. **Read Ephesians 2:10. Fill in the blanks.**

   "For we are God's workmanship, _____ in Christ Jesus to do _____ _____, which God prepared in _____ for us to do.

3. **What does this verse mean to you in everyday language?** _____
   _____

4. **Go to Psalm 40:5. Fill in the blanks:**

   "The things you _____ for us no one can recount to You; were I to speak and tell of them, they would be _____ _____ to declare."

5. **Psalm 25:12-13. Fill in the blanks.**

   "Who, then, is the man that _____ the Lord? He will _____ him in the way _____ for him. He will spend his days in _____ and his descendants will inherit the land."

6. **John 15:16. Fill in the blanks.**

   "You did not _____ Me, but I _____ you and appointed you to go and bear _____ that will last."

7. **Colossians 1:9 Fill in the blanks.**

   "…asking _____ to fill you with the knowledge of His _____ through all spiritual wisdom and understanding. And we pray this in order that you may live a _____ worthy of the Lord and may please Him in every way: bearing _____ in every good work and growing in the knowledge of God…

8. **Lastly, 1 Corinthians 2:9. Fill in the blanks.**

WEEK 1 | DAY 3

"No _____ has seen, no _____ has heard, no mind has _____ what God has prepared for those who _____ Him."

Are you beginning to see the good plans that God has ordained for those who are His? I've spent a good part of the last year and a half reading through a Chronological Bible. One of the common themes cover-to-cover is the good plan God has for those who say yes to Him. For those who love Him. For those who respond to His Word.

FAR TOO MANY CHRISTIANS, complete Step One by accepting Christ into their lives, but then never make God a major part of their lives. Yes, we may attend church each week. We may even serve in many different ways in our churches or communities. But if all we want is a little of Jesus to keep us out of hell, we are missing out on the fullness of life we were created for.

In addition, if we never engage in a meaningful relationship with the God of the universe by spending time with Him each day and discovering the great adventure He has planned for us in our *corner of the world, we settle for far less than what God wants to give us.*

JOURNAL RESPONSE

Take a few moments to meditate on our study today.

Were there particular Scripture(s) or statement(s) that spoke to you personally?

1.

2.

3.

WEEK 1 | DAY 4

TODAY'S TREASURE
...
"NO EYE HAS SEEN, NO EAR HAS HEARD, NO MIND HAS CONCEIVED WHAT GOD HAS PREPARED FOR THOSE WHO LOVE HIM."
1 Corinthians 2:9

YOUR LIFE IS NOT A SCARLET LETTER

Do you remember reading *The Scarlet Letter?* I read that novel in high school and I'll never forget it. The story is about a woman caught in adultery and forced to wear an obnoxious letter ("A" for adultery) on every piece of clothing. The intent was to bring shame and embarrassment. All would see and judge. She was forever left to care for her baby alone… discarded from society, family and friends; forever labeled "damaged goods."

As God allows me to travel and speak at women's conferences, one of the recurring themes I encounter is women living with searing loss or personal tragedy or guilt from their pasts. Unbeknownst to them, emotionally and spiritually, they are wearing their own scarlet letter.

Perhaps it's the scarlet letter of: D = divorce, A = adultery, addict, abortionist, abused, abandoned, abuser; F= fornicator, etc.

If we've been a victim of abuse or if we've been abandoned by a parent or spouse or fallen to various addictions, it's easy to think that God does not have a good plan for us.

If we have a past, as when Paul describes (himself) as *"the worst of sinners"*[28] – it's easy to think that God does not have a good plan for our lives, or that He could never use us for anything useful. We also tend to think our past exempts us from having a fruit-bearing life.

If we battle depression or disease or continual financial issues, it's very tempting to think that we are doomed to a life of misery; that nothing will ever change. The natural tendency is to label ourselves *"damaged goods."* So for some of you, the fact that God wants you to live a life of great purpose will require a titanic change in belief. However, please know, the Scriptures you studied yesterday **apply to you!** It's never too late for a fresh start – even if your life up to this point has been a train wreck.

A FRESH START

1. **Read Jeremiah 29:11. Fill in the blanks.** *"For I know the _____ I have for you,"* declares the Lord, *"plans to prosper you, and not to harm you, plans to give you _____ and a _____."*

---
[28] 1 Timothy 1:16

CREATED FOR PURPOSE

This is one of the most quotable verses found in the Bible. If you've been in church for any length of time, I'm quite sure you are familiar with this verse. But something we don't often realize is the context in which it was written. It was spoken through the prophet Jeremiah to the nation of Israel.

2. **Who are the people of Israel?** _____

In the Old Testament, Israel is God's beloved children.[29] Today, as New Testament people, God's children are those who have believed and received His Son, Jesus. The plans God had for His people then are the same plans He has for His children today. As we've seen from the Scriptures we've studied this week, God has a good plan *for those who belong to Him*.[30]

Yet, due to Israel's continual rebellion, their disregard, and their indifference to His Word, God's hand of protection was removed, and great hardship came upon them. The country of Babylon destroyed the beloved city of Jerusalem and carried His people into captivity far from their homeland and far from where God intended for them to be. So when God speaks this encouraging Word of hope to Jeremiah concerning Israel, God is in essence saying, *"I'll give you another chance. I want good for you – not bad. I want to give you a hope and a future. Will you cooperate with me?"*

The same is true for us. Sometimes choices are made for us that carry us far from where God intends for us to be. God is our Restorer and our Redeemer. He is able to restore the years the locusts have eaten, if we fully cooperate with Him.

At other times, we make choices that carry us far from where God desires us to be. Perhaps we choose to continually rebel or disregard God's Word in our everyday lives. Or we may go through the motions of religiosity and unknowingly become indifferent to God's Word, all of which takes us out of the will of God.

Think about a fenced-in back yard we have built for our children. That fenced-in area keeps our children safe and secure from the world-at-large. So it is with the Bible, God's Word. God's Word is a fence that keeps us safe and protected from the things He knows are bad or dangerous for us. When we choose to continually leave the safety of the fenced-in area, God doesn't stop us. He allows us to live as we choose.[31] However, there are consequences that come from living in rebellion and disregard of God's Word, things like depression, insecurity, financial misery, divorce, sexual diseases, obesity, and health problems.

3. **Name consequences I have not mentioned that occur when we CHOOSE to leave the fenced in area of God's will for our lives.**

_____

Yet just as God said to Israel, He says to us today, *"I'll give you another chance. I want good for you – not bad. I want to give you a hope and a future. Will you cooperate with me?"*

4. **What was the condition upon them having *"hope and a future?"* (See Jeremiah 29:13)**

_____

If we want our lives turned around, we can't give God lip service – telling Him we want Him to intervene; that we want change, yet stubbornly go on living the same way.

---

29 Israel was and is His chosen people from one man – Abraham. However, Israel as a nation has in large part rejected God's Son Jesus. John 1:10-11
30 He desires that every human being to know Him and belong to Him. 1 Timothy 2:4
31 Deuteronomy 30:19-20

WEEK 1 | DAY 4

Let's go into greater detail.

5. According to verse 12-13, what 4 things do we need to do in order to get God's attention?

_____, _____, _____ _____, _____

_____

6. What 3 things did God promise to do if they did their part? (v12-14)

_____, _____, _____,

Girlfriend, God has a **good plan** for our life. A plan of hope and a future! God is more than willing to do His part, however we must do our part as well.

What is our part? Our part is the same now as it was then for Israel: Call upon Him; come to Him; pray to Him; and seek Him with all our hearts. The amazing thing He promises: **He will be found and He will listen.** Is there anything greater in all the world than the Living God of the Universe promising to be found when we are in a pit so deep that we can't find our way out?

7. What hardship or pit are you in (or have you been in) as a result of living outside the fenced-in area of God's Word?

_____

8. What emotional or physical consequences have you experienced?

_____

9. Do you desire to be set free?

_____

If you are a woman who wears the invisible, perpetual Scarlet Letter – it's the enemy who's keeping it there, not God. God wants to set you free![32] He promises deliverance from the mess WE GOT OURSELVES INTO! However, we must fully cooperate with Him – on His terms – not ours.

If the invisible letter you are wearing is a result of your own sin, such as adultery or abortion, have you genuinely repented and allowed God to restore and redeem your failures? Genuine repentance is the first step to bringing complete and total forgiveness.[33] The guilt is removed and the sin is gone. God is ready to give you a fresh start!

Whether you made the mess yourself by poor choices, or poor choices were made for you, God wastes nothing in our lives. If you will seek God and work with Him in His way and in His time, God will take all that the enemy has meant for harm in your life and use it as a springboard for good[34]. He will carry you through with such a powerful story of deliverance that others will marvel at His activity in your life. And as a result, they will want to know your God![35]

The question is, will you allow Him to carry you and deliver you?

---

32 Isaiah 61:1
33 1 John 1:9
34 Genesis 50:20
35 Psalm 40:3

CREATED FOR PURPOSE

10. **Without giving God lip service, meaning answering yes to a question just because it sounds like the thing to say:**

    Are you willing to do your part? Are you willing to make tough decisions and stick with them in order to be free from your past? Are you willing to work hard emotionally and spiritually? Maybe even physically?

    _____

God has such amazing things planned for those of us who are His. Please do not shy away because you are afraid of what God might ask you to do. Perhaps you're afraid of what others may think. Or perhaps you just don't want to be physically and emotionally uncomfortable in social situations or any other situations. The longer we delay or ignore God's plan, the further we will be from His purpose for us.

For many years, I muddled through life wearing my own scarlet letter from my shameful past, not experiencing, *"no eye has seen, no ear has heard or mind conceived what God has planned for those who love Him."*

Not anymore. I've repented. I've worked with God, and I continue to work with God each day. Not on my terms, but on His terms. As a result, He's brought restoration and healing. He's removed the pain and the guilt from my past. I don't wear an invisible scarlet letter anymore. And every time the enemy tries to make me wear it by reminding me that *"I'm not worthy,"* I've learned to take authority over that lying voice in Jesus' name by telling the enemy that I'm a daughter of the King – healed and restored with a God-ordained purpose.

I'm here to say there's hope, girlfriend… Take off your scarlet letter and let's start living afresh!

JOURNAL RESPONSE

Take a few moments to meditate on our study today.

Were there particular Scripture(s) or statement(s) that spoke to you personally?

1.

2.

3.

REVIEW

1. What were the most meaningful or significant lessons you learned each day?

   Day 1: _____

   _____

   Day 2: _____

   _____

   Day 3: _____

   _____

   Day 4: _____

   _____

2. Is there anything you sense God telling you to do as a result of the study this week? If so, share.

   _____

   _____

3. What action steps do you need to take in order to be obedient?

   _____

   _____

2

MISLED BY A WORLD AND RELIGIOUS SYSTEM

WEEK TWO

Day 1 | Where Am I Going?

Day 2 | Have I Been Brainwashed?

Day 3 | Switching Paths

Day 4 | Sister Super Christian

Day 5 | Review

WEEK 2 | DAY 1

TODAY'S TREASURE
...
"STAND AT THE CROSSROADS AND LOOK; ASK FOR THE ANCIENT PATHS, ASK WHERE THE GOOD WAY IS AND WALK IN IT, AND YOU WILL FIND REST FOR YOUR SOULS."
JEREMIAH 6:16

Where Am I Going?

My grandmother used to live deep in rural North Carolina. On our way to her home, we would drive up to intersections in the road where all we could see were tobacco, cotton and soybean fields. I always wondered how my Dad knew where to go. All directions looked to the same to me. But they weren't. There was only one way to fried chicken, corn on the cob, tomatoes and green beans fresh from the garden, not to mention deviled eggs and potato salad. And for dessert, there would be chocolate pie, lemon pie, coconut pie, cherry pie, and German chocolate cake. (Seriously, she cooked all of it.)

Yet in order to make it to the promised land of good southern eatin', we had to navigate the roads deep in the country that, to me, all looked the same. A wrong turn would lead to another wrong turn and have ultimately taken us in a totally different direction and far from our goal.

So it is with life: so many paths to take, so many choices that look the same.

Read Jeremiah 6:16.

1. What does Jeremiah tell us we are to ask for? _____

2. What phrase describes the one thing most people long for? _____

3. Is this something you long for each day? _____

The ancient path can be described as the way of righteousness: Not righteousness according to our definition, but righteousness according to God's. Our soul include our mind, will and emotions. I've never met anyone who does not want rest for their mind, will and emotions. And I've never met anyone who does not want their life to have eternal significance. Yet in life, there are so many paths to choose from for daily living. But according to the Bible, the bottom line is this: In God's eyes, there are only three paths to choose from. Today, we will examine those three paths.

PATH #1: UNBELIEVERS JUDGMENT

Read Revelation 20:11-15

CREATED FOR PURPOSE

Just as I needed a map or guide to get me to my grandmother's house, we have been given a map for living called the Bible. Many people ignore this map by trying to figure out life on their own. Those who ignore and disregard the contents of this map will one day be very sorry.

4. What event is happening in this passage? (v11) _____

5. Who is being judged? (v12) _____

6. What criteria is used for judgment? (12c) _____

7. What is the name of the primary *"book"* referred to in this passage? (15)
   _____

8. What is vital to avoid, *"the lake of fire?"* _____

This is a very sobering passage of Scripture. Moments before Jesus' ascension, He says, "…whoever does not believe will be condemned." This is a description of the condemnation Jesus spoke of. It's the end of an unbeliever's path that leads to the *"Great White Throne Judgment."* When people reject Jesus as Savior, they will carry their sins into death. God takes sin very seriously.[1] God sent Jesus to stand in our place for the punishment of our sin. Jesus became sin, so that you and I didn't have to carry the consequences of our sin into death. Our sin can be placed upon Jesus so that what we are reading in this passage does not happen to us. But let's be clear, this WILL HAPPEN[2] to those who reject God's Way (Jesus) into His heaven. Sadly, this is the path that most are walking upon because they refuse to acknowledge Jesus. The Bible, our Map, gives us very clear direction on how this path ends.

Also notice that it says that those who reject Jesus will be held accountable *"for what they have done."* It is a very grim picture of torment that will last forever as the second death occurs when they are thrown into the lake of fire.

HOWEVER, when you and I make the decision to invite Jesus into our life, our names are written in the Book of Life. Whew! Are you breathing a sigh of relief? If you are a child of God, the Great White Throne Judgment is not your destiny.

However, the end path for believers is another kind of judgment. It's based upon how we lived our lives while on planet Earth. Let's take a look at how our Map describes it.

PATH #2: BELIEVERS JUDGMENT SEAT

Read 2 Corinthians 5:10

9. Who will appear before the judgment seat of Christ? _____

10. What will we receive? _____
    _____

Every single human being will stand before Christ one day to give an account for the way we lived our lives. We just read about the judgment for unbelievers. However, I want you to note that in this particular

---

1   Despite the fact that this world takes sin very lightly, we must not be deceived that God turns a blind eye to sin. He does not.
2   You will never read this warning in a newspaper; a magazine article or hear it on television. The wise will take heed. Matthew 7:14

WEEK 2 | DAY 1

passage, Paul is speaking to the **believers**: Those who have become children of God and whose names are found in the Book of Life.

Let's continue to more understanding…

PATH #2 & 3: BELIEVERS JUDGEMENT SEAT

Read 1 Corinthians 3:10-15

11. What event is being described in this passage? _____

12. What is meant by *"each one should be careful how he builds?"* (v10)

_____

Paul is describing the day of judgment and is telling us from the onset that we should be careful how we build our lives. This passage has nothing to do with losing salvation.[3]

13. What is the foundation of our life to be? (v11) _____

14. What elements should we add to that foundation? (v12a)

_____

15. In broad terms, what does the gold, silver, and costly stones represent? (12)

_____

16. In broad terms, what do the wood, hay and straw represent?

_____

17. What will test the quality of each man's work?

_____

18. What will happen if it survives? (14) _____

19. What happens if the way you spent your life burns up? (v15)

_____

We will ALL be held accountable for the way we lived our lives during our tenure on Earth. For example: the way we raised our children – did we raise them to know and love the Lord with all their heart, mind and soul, or did we raise them to have worldly goals only? The way we treated our spouse; the way we treated other people; the choices we've made; the priorities we lived; the way we spent our money; how we've spent our time. Not only that, but we will be held accountable for how we responded to God and His Word.

Jesus is to be the foundation of our lives. When we add gold, silver and costly stones to that foundation, we can be sure that our lives will be of great value before the Lord. We will be a success in God's eyes as the gold, silver and costly stones represent THE ANCIENT PATH. It is the good path; the righteous

---

[3] Romans 8:9-11; Revelation 20:12,15

path. Not only that, it's the only path that brings rest to our souls. For gold, silver and costly stones are valuable and enduring.

However, the Bible indicates that if we make poor life choices in the eyes of Him Who matters, we are building our lives using wood, straw, and hay. This includes placing importance on accolades, achievements and accomplishments that we thought would matter or bring importance in eternity will actually burn when tested by fire. As one of my dearly loved Bible teachers once taught me, *"We can have a saved soul, but will live a wasted life."*

This is important: we can be a huge success in the eyes of the world. Yet be a failure in the eyes of God. And in the end, despite the success we may have enjoyed during our lives, it will count for NOTHING in eternity.

So over next few days, we will investigate what the *wood, the straw and the hay* represent in everyday life. I want you to even know what these things smell like, for surely they are what stands in the way of having the life God desires to give us. Starting next week, we'll dig deeper into what gold, silver and costly stones look like in our everyday life. For certainly, when we embrace what Scripture calls gold, silver and costly stones, we begin to truly live a life that has great significance.

The two paths **believers** can take:

Path #1: The path of gold, silver and costly stones. (By the way, it does not represent jewelry.)

Path #2: The path of wood, hay and straw – Brainwashed Boulevard.

JOURNAL RESPONSE

Take a few moments to meditate on our study today.

Were there particular Scripture(s) or statement(s) that spoke to you personally?

1.

2.

3.

WEEK 2 | DAY 2

TODAY'S TREASURE
...
"YOU LET THE WORLD, WHICH DOESN'T KNOW THE FIRST THING ABOUT LIVING, TELL YOU HOW TO LIVE."
EPHESIANS 2:2 (MSG. TRANSLATION)

HAVE I BEEN BRAINWASHED?

As we begin our lesson today, we will see why so many take this path, whether they are believers or unbelievers. To be honest, you will like this path! And the majority of the people we probably know and work with and possibly go to church with are on this path.

Although this path looks good, make no mistake: when we build our lives upon the items we'll find on this path, we are merely building our lives upon wood, hay and straw. Because of its allure, we'll call this path: Brainwashed Boulevard.

Brainwashed Boulevard represents all the world holds dear. But it will not take us to the ending point we desire. Its promises are empty and will never bring rest to our souls or genuine purpose to our lives. This lesson is not meant to impugn anyone or anything. You see, the things we will talk about today **are not bad things**. On the contrary, **they are really good things**. But the dividing line is a matter of possession. Do we possess them or do they possess us?

DEFINITION OF SUCCESS

1. **How does our culture define a person who is successful?** _____
_____

A few years ago, my mother was shopping at the local mall and ran into the mother of one of my friends from high school. The last time she had seen this woman was 20 years ago, at our graduation. As moms often do, they shared their children's accomplishments and accolades - regardless of age!

As Mom recalled the encounter, she said the woman talked non-stop about all her adult children had accomplished – a master's degree, career promotions, new houses in the town's most affluent neighborhood, grandchildren who were A/B Honor Roll students... The list went on and on. While Mom was thrilled, she was running late and desperately needed to graciously exit the conversation[4].

---

[4] She later told me that she was disappointed she didn't have an opportunity to share what my sister, Heather and I are doing. We giggled at the thought of how the woman would have responded had Mom said, *"Well my girls are serving the Lord with all their heart and making a difference in their small corners of the world! Let me tell you what all they are doing…"*

It's funny how success is defined. According the world's standards and from all outward appearances, my high school friend and her sibling have it all: wealth, success and prosperity. It would seem that they are living the life![5]

Now, let's connect the *wood, the straw and the hay* from yesterday's lesson to the world's definition of success and how easily we begin to make it our *definition of success*.

DEEMED TO MATTER

Let's face it, most of the world is obsessed with stuff! Stuff like wealth, celebrity, sports, fitness, and royalty, just to name a few things. The general message constantly communicated through ads, television, books and movies is: *"If we strive to obtain the things that are deemed to matter in life, then we too, will be living a life that counts, a life of great significance; We will have satisfaction, joy, meaning and purpose. Happiness is finally within our grasp. That we'll have it all! We will have reached the nirvana of life!"*

Your list may have included:

- Building our bank account; our portfolio
- Striving for the bigger house; a more affluent neighborhood
- A second or third home
- Boats and cars
- Greater education
- The perfect physique
- Trendy clothes, shoes, and handbags
- Climbing the corporate latter
- A perfectly decorated home
- Raising perfect, well-mannered, well-educated children
- Social acceptance with peers
- Marrying well
- The more vacations, the better
- Skillfully juggling kids, work, service, a social life, and contributing something to the world
- World peace!

Remember, **there is <u>NOTHING</u> WRONG** with the above list. NOTHING! Now before you think that I'm the fun police, hear me out... To many Believers, *this is <u>all</u> that matters in life.* The world has a way of warping our perspective and making us think that it's the <u>**ONLY**</u> **thing that matters in life, that this is what makes our lives a success. That's why this path is called Brainwashed Boulevard.**

We can be a success in the eyes of the world, but fail in the eyes of God. Despite all the accolades and rewards people collect during their earthly lives, one of the most important things that matters at the moment

---

[5] Please note, I know nothing about their hearts. This is merely an illustration of how success is defined in our culture.

of death is what they did in obedience to God's Word. That's it! Everything else, without exception, will be no more.

REPROGRAMMED

2. Read Luke 12:15. What are we to be on guard against? _____

   a. Why? (15b) _____

Yet what is the message we hear from TV, movies, ads, and almost everything else in the world? *That life is measured by how much you own. That a person's worth is based upon what they own.*

Read Luke 12:21 NLT, *"Yes, a person is a fool to store up earthly wealth but not have a rich relationship with God."*

3. What is success in the eyes of God? _____

4. Describe what it means to have a rich relationship with God.
   _____

First of all, if I'm not careful, Brainwashed Boulevard is a street I automatically turn towards. For years following college, I was the poster child for Brainwashed Boulevard. You see, the list from above is my list. The things on this list were the *only things I focused on in life*.

Yes, I had a little of Jesus in my life. Yes, I went to church each weekend. Yes, I was in Bible study. But God was an add-on to a very busy life. My marriage? I wasn't focused on making my marriage a happy, thriving relationship. I was focused on how my husband could best serve me. And if he wasn't focused on me and my needs, I tended to be angry. I was very self-absorbed.

My mind needed to be redirected… reprogrammed. My focus was all wrong.

5. **Are you currently strolling down Brainwashed Boulevard, or was there a time in your life when you found yourself walking along this alluring path? Share with your group.**
   _____

6. Read Colossians 3:2. Where should we set our minds? _____

7. **Jeremiah 9:23-24. Fill in the blanks:**

   "Let not the wise man boast of his _____, or the strong man boast of his _____, or the rich man boast of his _____, but let him who boasts boast about this: that he understands and _____ Me, that I am the Lord… for in these I delight," **declares the Lord.**

Understanding and knowing God; having a rich relationship with God: This is all that matters in life. Yes, we can have all the world allows us to obtain, but apart from a rich relationship with Jesus – it's wood and it's straw and it's hay! It will burn when we stand before Him Who counts. And apart from a rich relationship with Jesus, none of the things that the world gives us will bring deep-down peace to our souls.

8. In whose eyes do you want to be a success? _____

9. **Look at today's treasure. In what ways have you allowed the world, which doesn't know the first thing about living, tell you how to live?**

   _____

I hope and pray you've resolved to want to be a success in the eyes of God. To be a success in God's eyes is to live a fruitful life – a life of meaning and purpose! For those of you who identify with being brainwashed by a very alluring world and desire to be a success in God's eyes, hang on. You may need to switch paths.

JOURNAL RESPONSE

Take a few moments to meditate on our study today.

Were there particular Scripture(s) or statement(s) that spoke to you personally?

1.

2.

3.

WEEK 2 | DAY 3

TODAY'S TREASURE
...
"YES, A PERSON IS A FOOL TO STORE UP EARTHLY WEALTH BUT NOT HAVE A RICH RELATIONSHIP WITH GOD."
LUKE 12:21 (NLT)

SWITCHING PATHS

You've worked hard this week. For some of you, you've been asked to ingest hard truth with thought-provoking Scripture. For others, it has been a reminder of where NOT to set our minds despite the allure of all the world has to offer; a reminder to not allow our lives to be defined by what we own, but instead to strive to be rich in relationship with God.

And remember, it's not that the things of the world are necessarily evil – it's a matter of? _____[6]

Let's review our week thus far:

1. **What is one name for the path that is very alluring to believers and unbelievers alike?**

   _____

2. **Why do most people walk down this path?**

   _____

3. **What path does the Bible say we should ask for?**

   _____

4. **Why are we to ask for this path?** _____

5. **What again is our overall goal?**

   _____

The *"ancient path"* of righteousness is our goal. Not perfection, but intentionally building our lives using gold, silver and costly stones. This path requires spending time with God and having a rich relationship with Him. It's the path that will lead us to bear eternal fruit. It's the path that will help us to not only find rest for our souls, but find all that God desires to give us while living on planet Earth!

---

[6] Hint: Who possesses whom?

When our lives bear fruit, the Bible promises that our lives will have meaning and purpose. Our lives will have significance. Not only that, but we will stand before the Lord at the end of our lives unashamed, with no regrets.

Let's continue our review:

6. **When we stand before Jesus at the end of our lives, how are** *"things of the world"* **described?**

    1 Corinthians 3:12: _____

7. **In your opinion, what often causes us to want to switch to the ancient path?**

    _____

The reason for the path or life perspective change will be different for each of us. Today, I'd like to share my reasons. One of the things I want you to see through my story is that things are not as they may seem. You see, looking from the outside in, you would have thought I had it all.

In high school, I had lots of friends. I was a cheerleader, and even homecoming queen my senior year. I had a new car – an '87 Ford Mustang, which was really awesome. I had a great boyfriend whom I would one day marry. I had a wonderful family who was actively engaged in every part of my life. I was an honor roll student. And for the most part, I toed the line. I never got into any real trouble. (Please know, this does not mean I was flawless.)

For the most part, this looks pretty good from the outside, doesn't it? Keep reading!

Sadly, during my high school and college years, I walked further and further away from the God I was raised to know. I lived a fairly moral life according to the world's terms. But it wasn't enough. There was still something missing on the inside of me.

However, at the same time, I saw something different happening in my mother. Her faith was coming alive. And during college, she was the rock I leaned upon – especially when my heart was broken. I'd call her from school in tears. She always knew just what to say to make me feel better. She encouraged me and gave me good practical advice without judging me or coming out of her skin. (Looking back, she exercised such great restraint!)

Following college graduation, I moved back to my home town. Again, from the outside looking in, it looked good. I lived in the premier location in my city. I had a good job and a cool car; I still had the same great guy – But it wasn't enough. Something was missing.

I desperately yearned for the same deep-down peace and joy my mother possessed. But I continued with my own *"add-on"* mentality, meaning that, for me at that time, God was an add-on to an already busy life. I made time for Him and church when it was convenient.

The restlessness within my spirit compelled me to enroll in the Bible study that Mom had been a part of for so many years. I instinctively knew the missing element in my life was my relationship with Jesus. It had been long abandoned. More than that, it had been compromised in exchange for all the world deemed important for far too many years.

TURNING AROUND

8. **Read Isaiah 48:17.**

WEEK 2 | DAY 3

    a. Who directs us in the way we should go? _____

    b. What else according to verse 17 does He do? _____

    c. According to verse 18, what did not happen? _____

    d. What were the blessings forfeited as a result? (v18) _____

9. Has there ever been a time in your life that you would have said this verse describes you? If so, share if it's not too personal. _____
_____

10. What caused you to want to switch paths? Or are you still trying to figure out whether you need to switch paths? (Briefly explain)
_____
_____

Oh, the blessings that I forfeited because I wanted to walk the way of the world on Brainwashed Boulevard! I wanted to fit in – I wanted to be liked. And though I was like any college student you might observe from the outside, I inwardly knew I was *lookin' for love in all the wrong places:* in bars, through relationships, through friends, through social prominence, etc. Many days I ignored the voice inside, which was the Holy Spirit warning me[7], trying to redirect me toward the ancient path – the better way, the good path.

I marvel at the love of the Lord as I look back. With every step, I was walking further and further away from God, yet He was clinging ever tightly to me. Never letting me go, yet allowing me to reap the consequences of leaving His will for my life.

11. Can you identify? Briefly share: _____

12. What consequences were reaped during this season? _____

Though the Lord never let me go, this does not mean that He did not allow me to reap the consequences of my godless lifestyle. I was riddled with insecurity and perpetual feelings of inferiority. Instead of peace in my heart, I became anxious and discontent. Everyone around me seemed to have so much more. I always felt trapped by my limited resources that I so foolishly wasted, and I could never be alone. If I were alone, I'd have to hear the conviction of the Lord in my heart. I didn't want to hear what I already knew to be true deep in my heart, so I ran from His voice by busying myself with activity, people, TV – anything so I didn't have to be alone, hearing the quiet voice of my Savior calling me back.

To this day, I can't ride through the city I went to college in without those feelings flooding my heart – but at the same time, I thank God for it!

Inward misery and discontent is what ultimately brought me back into His loving arms. You see, He KNEW what He had planned for this little child of His. Our infinite God is not bound by the constraints of time and space, so He could see what I would and (will) ultimately become. He never gave up on me. I had a call on my life. **So do you, sweet friend.**

---

[7] I didn't realize it was His voice at the time, but looking back, He was there. John 16:13. The Holy Spirit is our Guide.

CREATED FOR PURPOSE

13. How does Romans 11:29 reiterate this fact? _____

Every believer in Jesus Christ has God-given gifts and a calling upon their lives that is irrevocable. It will never be taken away. However, these gifts and callings may lie dormant if we never identify and engage them. One of the keys to abundant living and living a life of great purpose is found in identifying and engaging these gifts and callings upon our lives. This is a subject that you will see developed in later weeks. But I want to plant the seed now, for it will be one of the catalysts that enables us to have and enjoy our lives (living on the ancient path) – allowing us to be fruitful in our corner of the world.[8]

14. Who has God placed in your life that has served as a catalyst for you to want to know their Jesus firsthand? _____

My mom's peace, joy and stability made me want her Jesus. It wasn't that she was at church every time the doors were opened. She was different. She and my father loved me unconditionally. They didn't seem to judge me, but accepted me. This does not mean they accepted my lifestyle choices. They always stood firm on godly principles.

Often God will do this. He'll strategically place someone in your life that represents the very thing your soul craves. You see, we were made to crave Him. He knows just how to get our attention. The question is: are we paying attention? Are we listening to the *"One who teaches us what is best for us, Who directs us in the way we should go"*?

JOURNAL RESPONSE

Take a few moments to meditate on our study today.

Were there particular Scripture(s) or statement(s) that spoke to you personally?

1.

2.

3.

---

8   John 10:10; John 15:1-17

WEEK 2 | DAY 4

TODAY'S TREASURE
...
"DO NOT CONSIDER HIS OUTWARD APPEARANCE... FOR I HAVE REJECTED HIM. THE LORD DOES NOT LOOK AT THE THINGS MAN LOOKS AT. MAN LOOKS AT THE OUTWARD APPEARANCE, BUT THE LORD LOOKS AT THE HEART."
1 Samuel 16:7

SISTER SUPER CHRISTIAN

Today, I'd like to introduce you to "Sister Super Christian." She is a church girl. Many of you will like her. Many of you may identify with her. She's sweet. She has a good heart and great intentions. Sister Super Christian is very impressive.

She can quote Scriptures from memory;
    She attends church regularly and is familiar with denominational traditions and rituals.
        She can often sing hymns or praise songs from memory as well.
            She's comfortable going to Bible study –
                She may even go on an overseas Mission trip.
She's REALLY AWESOME! From all outward appearances – she's got it going on.

1. From Today's Scripture, what does man look at? _____

2. What does the Lord look at? _____

3. What does it mean to *"look at the heart"*? _____
_____

This Scripture goes hand-in-hand with Brainwashed Boulevard. Someone and their activities can look really good on the outside. Yet, only God sees what truly lies within. He knows the thoughts, the plans and the motives of the heart.

John 15 is familiar as we read this during Week 1. However, today, I want you to keep something in mind as you approach this passage: these were some of the last instructions Jesus gave to His disciples.[9] He knew the Cross was a day away; He knew that following His death, burial and resurrection, that His time on planet Earth would be limited. He was giving last instructions to the 12 people whom He poured His

---
[9] John 13-16 is where we find Jesus' final instructions to His disciples.

life into. He was telling them how to live in the next season of their lives. To focus on what was important and eternal – not what was temporary and worthless.

4. **Read John 15:1-8.**

    a. **Who is the Gardener?** _____

    b. **Who is the Vine?** _____

    c. **Who are the branches?** _____

    d. **What does "remain in Me," mean?**

    _____

    _____

    e. **What does "bear much fruit," mean to you?**

    _____

    _____

5. **Read John 15:8. What does God *"glory in?"*** _____

6. **Read John 15:16. What is our primary function in life?** _____

7. **What kind of fruit?** _____

Prior to 2004, I would have characterized my relationship with God as strong. I was learning a great deal in the Bible study I spoke of yesterday, so I wanted to serve! I was at church every Sunday morning and was serving fervently. I was the Prayer Committee Chairperson - which was a big commitment that required prayer with the Ministers prior to Sunday service and often meetings and events outside of Sunday.

Twice a week I attended an in-depth Bible study of which I was a small group leader of 15 women. This commitment required at least 15 hours of my time each week. I also taught 4th grade Sunday School. Not only that, but I could recite the Lord's Prayer, the Apostle's Creed and many Bible verses from memory. I was friends with the ministers of my church and was part of their leadership team. In my community, I was friends with many women who were active in ministry.

Ok, so maybe I wasn't just the poster child for Sister Super Christian…I was Sister Super-Christian.

8. From all appearances, was my life fruitful? _____

Looks good from the outside doesn't it? Many would call this a fruitful life… Only the Gardner (God) truly knows if there was genuine fruit being produced during this particular season. However, because of what the Lord has taught me, minimal fruit at best was being produced during this period of time. Why? Because only the Gardner could see the heart and what was happening privately.

WEEK 2 | DAY 4

PRIVATELY

Privately, behind closed doors where only my family and God could see:[10]
>My marriage was in disarray due to my busyness in Christian service.
>My home was often in chaos and my children had a schedule of their own.
>I tried consistently to be the head of the home.[11]
>We could never go to church as a family because I was
>too busy SERVING. We drove separately.

In addition, I was often consumed with anger, bitterness, and resentment towards my husband. Oh the Sunday mornings I would put on my Sunday morning face and sing praise songs as if the silence between us didn't exist.

Not only that, I had issues with self-righteousness and pride because I deemed myself to be so important spiritually. I loved to be seen serving.

Most importantly, and I do say MOST IMPORTANTLY, my quiet time was rote and mechanical at best. My prayer life was shallow; My Bible study mentality was that lessons we covered were for *other people*, not personally applied or personally transformational. Without personal application and allowing the Word to change and transform *MY* heart (first) and then *them*[12], I was merely going through the motions of religiosity. I had only the appearance of fruit – the appearance of a life using the elements of gold, silver and costly stones – the appearance of a life on the Ancient Path.

It nauseates me to share these things with you. I hope it's helping you. If you can identify with any part of my story, than it's time to wake up! God sees the heart. He can see motives; He can see self-righteousness and pride.

9. Relate Today's Scripture to the story above. What were the disconnects in my life during this time? What are the disconnects in your own life? _____

_____

BRAINWASHED BY RELIGION

"These people say they are Mine. They honor Me with their lips, but their hearts are far from Me. And their worship of Me is nothing but man-made rules learned by rote." Isaiah 29:13 (NTL)

10. Fill in the blanks. Isaiah 29:13 NLT

> *"These people say they are _____. They honor Me with their*
> *_____, but their _____ are far from Me."*

Ouch! Talk about a scathing rebuke, yet it's epidemic in the worldwide church of Jesus Christ. Lips that honor Him; lips that say we belong to Him, but hearts that are far from Him.

Our physical bodies can be at church every time the doors are opened, yet we can have hearts that are far from Him.

---
10 I had 2 small children and a husband.
11 God's best is for the man to be the head of the home. 1 Peter 3:1
12 The *them* was typically for my husband, not me!

CREATED FOR PURPOSE

We can know all the Christian things to say, such as, *"Praise the Lord;" "I'll pray for you;"* and *"What a blessing."*
    Yet we can have hearts that are far from Him.
We can give countless hours planning women's events and functions in His name.
    Yet we can have hearts that are far from Him...
We can feed the poor; clothe the naked; house the homeless
    Yet have hearts that are far from His perspective and far from His priorities for our lives.

To remain or abide on the Vine **does not mean** to remain in church or religious activities the majority of the time. Just as a vine provides nourishment to the branches, Jesus is to be our daily nourishment. To remain and to abide in Him means to cultivate an ever-growing relationship by spending time with Him in prayer and Bible study. It is in this time that He guides us and directs us for our everyday lives and enables us through the power of His Spirit living within us to be fruitful in our corners of the world. This is when we begin **"to live and move and have our being in Him,"** as Paul says in Acts 17:28. Yet all too often in Christian circles, busyness serving replaces the vital necessity of time *spent with* God and getting to know Him personally.

We must also understand that if we are not careful, we can be so busy going to Bible study and having a quiet time of same shape or form, yet fail to take God's word personally. **We may fail to allow the Word to permeate and transform our hearts, our thinking, our actions, and our behavior. One failure builds on another, so that we ultimately fail to live God's purpose in our families, friends, communities and churches: in other words, in all the places that God desires us to be fruitful and to have significant impact for Him.**

There is a fix for Super Sister Christian. Hang tight. We'll soon find out what that fix is. But for now, I'm praying that you'll become aware if Sister Super Christian exists in you.

REVIEW

11. What often replaces time spent with God? _____

12. During our time with God, what should we be allowing the Word to do?

13. Can you in anyway identify with Sister Super Christian? Explain

_____

_____

If you answered yes, take heart. There's no condemnation in Christ.[13] Perhaps He's led you to this study for such a time as this, for the same paradigm shift I too so desperately needed.

Sadly, the flip to Sister Super Christian can happen as well. Because of religious zeal, you may have fallen victim to Sister Super Christian, just as my husband did. When this happens, nothing in us wants anything to do with that person's Jesus.

14. Have you possibly been turned off of Jesus because of a Sister Super Christian in your corner of the world? _____

---
13   Romans 8:1

WEEK 2 | DAY 4

If you answered yes, from the bottom of my heart, I'm so very sorry that we've misrepresented who Jesus really is. Please know that Sister Super Christian has good intentions, but will often unintentionally misrepresent Jesus and who He really is.

Why? Because she knows religion or denominational rules from heart, yet she has not taken the time to know Jesus. Take it from me. There is no telling how many people I negatively impacted. If I'm not careful, I could do so even now. Lord, help me!

The bottom line: We are each called to produce authentic fruit, fruit that will last. We are called to lead fruitful lives so that when we stand before Jesus, *"on that day,"* we will hear the words, **"Well done, good and faithful servant. You have been faithful with a few things; I will put you in charge of many things. Come and share your Master's happiness!"**[14]

This will not happen if we live by a Sister Super Christian or a "Church Girl" mentality. It will require us to think differently, to behave differently, to have a different mentality.

We will need to become Jesus girls.

JOURNAL RESPONSE

Take a few moments to meditate on our study today.

Were there particular Scripture(s) or statement(s) that spoke to you personally?

1.

2.

3.

---

14   Matthew 25:21

REVIEW

1. What were the most meaningful or significant lessons you learned each day?

   Day 1: _____
   _____

   Day 2: _____
   _____

   Day 3: _____
   _____

   Day 4: _____
   _____

2. Is there anything you sense God telling you to do as a result of the study this week? If so, share.

   _____
   _____

3. What action steps do you need to take in order to be obedient?

   _____
   _____

3

THE CHURCH GIRL AND THE JESUS GIRL

WEEK THREE

- Day 1 | The Church Girl and the Jesus Girl
- Day 2 | Church Girl or Jesus Girl
- Day 3 | The Jesus Girl
- Day 4 | Church Girl to Jesus Girl
- Day 5 | Review

WEEK 3 | DAY 1

TODAY'S TREASURE
...
"I KNOW YOUR DEEDS; YOU HAVE
A REPUTATION FOR BEING ALIVE,
BUT YOU ARE DEAD. WAKE UP!"
REVELATION 3:1

THE CHURCH GIRL AND THE JESUS GIRL

Today, we are going to continue our journey of understanding the reality of "Sister Super Christian," aka the "church girl." Please know ahead of time, this is not an indictment of the church. Actually, this will bless the body of Jesus Christ, because when we kick our church girl mentality to the curb and radically embrace the "Jesus Girl" mentality, the church in our corners of the world will look totally different.

First let's look at Jesus' acknowledgement of the church girl and His warning to her. This verse is important, especially if you are a leader in any way shape or form in the Body of Christ. If so, memorize this verse. Meditate on it and never forget it.

1. **Read Revelation 3:1b.**

    a. **What deeds do you think Jesus is speaking of?** _____

    _____

    b. **What does a reputation for being alive mean?** _____

    _____

    c. **What does the phrase, "but you are dead," mean?** _____

    _____

Jesus is not speaking to unbelievers in this passage. He's speaking to the church of Sardis. They had a reputation for being alive spiritually, but in fact, they were spiritually dead. Not spiritual or physical deadness, but deadness in terms of their love and passion for Jesus. Their relationship had become mechanical, rote, perhaps legalistic. They knew all the right phrases and clichés; they were far more concerned with impressing others than God Himself. Despite this devastating charge, Jesus wanted them to change. It wasn't too late.

    d. **What does He tell them to do? (v2a)** _____

Sweet friend, this study is written to wake us up to the life that Jesus has planned for each of us. He has a good plan. He is our Creator and created us for good works, placing within each of us amazing gifts. He has strategically placed us in our corners of the world for impact. Yet we must lean upon Him and choose to do life His way. Oh the blessings that come when we do!

CREATED FOR PURPOSE

I want to personally confess that if I'm not careful, the rebuke addressed to the church in Sardis could be addressed to me in any given season. It's easy to drift into spiritual complacency or to go through the motions of religion, allowing our faith to grow stale and mediocre. Why? Because when we attend church or Bible Study, we automatically think we are *"alive,"* spiritually astute, growing in our knowledge of the Bible **academically**. What's more, we have a reputation of being *"alive"* to the people we work with, to our extended family, to our neighbors, friends, and acquaintances because they know we are in Bible Study or serving God. How easy to think we are alive because of our deeds. But in actuality, we've become deluded by our own significance.

2. **What 2 things does Jesus say do in Revelation 3:2?** _____ (2a)

   _____ (2b)

3. **What are the steps to** *"waking up,"* **according to Revelation 3:3?**

   a. _____

   b. _____

   c. _____

Jesus makes it so simple to come back to Him. But the *first step to waking up is to repent. The second step is to remember* what we have received and heard during our time with Jesus:

> In our quiet time;
>   At church on Sunday morning;
>   At our women's Bible Study each week;
> At conferences;
>   Through our mentors and Jesus friends;
> And the third step is to obey what He impresses upon your heart to do.[1]

---

[1] This is where the Prayer Journal, *Intimacy with God; Your Daily Guide to Prayer* has helped me so much. I write down what I sense Jesus saying to me from my time with Him. This helps me to remember and to obey.

WEEK 3 | DAY 1

THE CHURCH GIRL/JESUS GIRL DIFFERENCES

After examining my own heart, the Lord revealed the Church Girl mentality to me. This revelation was a wakeup call for me personally. Below is a chart of practical ways to *"Wake up"* and begin embracing the Jesus Girl mentality.

CHURCH GIRL	JESUS GIRL
Goes to church or Bible Study each week, but her life is not different.	Her life is progressively becoming more Christ-like as she personally applies what she's learning in church and Bible Study
Flavor of the week mentality – each lesson is a great lesson for that week! But it is soon forgotten because she learns another great lesson the next week. The problem is that there's no personal application.	Lifestyle change – each lesson is being studied, written down, and applied to her everyday life. She makes each lesson a catalyst for lifestyle change, not just the flavor of the week.
She knows all about God.	She knows God personally.
She's not growing in her relationship with God because she spends very little time with Him. What time she does spend is rote.	She's growing in her relationship because she makes spending time with God a priority.
Her approach to Bible study is often academic.	Her approach to study is personal.
Lives a compartmentalized life. She has church friends or Bible Study friends and then another "personality" for other friends.	Jesus is her life.
She may possibly not be a child of God – because not everyone serving in our churches is a born again believer. She can't remember when she made the personal decision to invite Jesus into her heart.	Is a child of God and can vividly remember when she personally invited Him into her life.
She's memorized hymns, the Apostles Creed, the Lord's Prayer and has many Scripture verses memorized – but it's all in her head.	The words in the hymns, the Apostles Creed, the Lord's Prayer and the Scriptures are not just idle words. They govern her behavior, motives, and decisions in life.
If Scripture challenges her lifestyle or current belief system, she hardens her heart and refuses to shift in the direction the Holy Spirit may be leading.	Her heart is pliable and moldable towards Scripture, even when that means being left out of strategic social relationships or contradicting lifestyles around her.
She tends to look down on others who are not as spiritual or as educated as she is.	She's very humble towards everyone, realizing that were it not for the grace of God, she would be adrift, too.
She tends to think she knows everything, that there's nothing new she can be taught.	She's hungry to learn more about the Word.
People-based, Leader-based, Pastor-based – Follows a Bible Study teacher or leader and may have elevated that leader to "god-like" status.	Word based.
Is taught something from the pulpit and never questions it.	Is like the Bereans – she examines the Scriptures to see if what she's been taught is actually true.
Casual approach to Bible study and Church. Does not think or know if she'll hear from God when she attends each week. It's just what she does each Sunday.	She comes to church and Bible Study expecting to hear a personal Word from God.
She's a woman of action. She sees a need and jumps to it!	She sees a need and goes to prayer. If confirmed in prayer – she takes it to her husband for his approval. (If married.) Only with God's confirmation and that of her husband does she jump to action.

CREATED FOR PURPOSE

CHURCH GIRL	JESUS GIRL
Has a shallow prayer life	Has a growing, vibrant prayer life
Goes to friends – even godly friends for help.	Goes first to Jesus in prayer and His Word for help, and then to godly women if led.
Her power for service is in her own strength because she's too busy serving to find quality time alone with Jesus.	Her power is supernatural because she embodies John 15.
Not eternally fruitful	VERY fruitful

4. What are your thoughts on the Church girl vs. the Jesus Girl?

   _____

   _____

   _____

5. Which descriptions stand out most?

   _____

6. Do you identify with one over the other?

   _____

7. Are there any changes you need to make to your personal life following today's lesson?

   Where do you need to start?

   _____

   Then what do you sense Jesus telling you to do?

   _____

JOURNAL RESPONSE

Take a few moments to meditate on our study today.

Were there particular Scripture(s) or statement(s) that spoke to you personally?

1.

2.

3.

WEEK 3 | DAY 2

TODAY'S TREASURE
...
"I KNOW YOUR DEEDS,
YOUR HARD WORK AND
PERSEVERANCE... YOU HAVE
FORSAKEN YOUR FIRST LOVE..."
REVELATION 2:2,4

CHURCH GIRL? JESUS GIRL?

Several years ago, I was invited to be on a Task Force that would put together a Women's Ministry for a very large denomination that was wise enough to know they NEEDED a formal women's ministry. It was such an honor to be asked to serve. The commitment lasted for two years. At the end of the two years, a director would be hired and the Task Force would be dissolved.

Just before the formal hiring of the director, we organized a Fellowship and Training for Women's Ministry Leaders representing many churches throughout my state. I was SO EXCITED! I love being around women who are wiser, more discerning and further in their walk than me. I'm like a sponge and want to soak in their Jesus wisdom.

The event was attended by hundreds of women. I worked the event and was assigned to move from table to table and listen to the concerns that these women's ministry leaders encounter in their churches.

Would you believe that with the exception of one woman at one table, Jesus was nowhere to be found that day? There was no discussion of prayer, of Bible reading, or hearing the Lord's direction in their ministries. This event might as well have been a civic club function.

My heart was broken for the women these ministry leaders represented.

1. **Read John 20:13. Fill in the blanks.** *"They have taken my _____ away," she said, "and I don't know where they have _____ _____."*

2. **Who had been taken away?** _____

3. **How does John 20:13 connect with what we've learned about the Church girl?**
   _____

Just as Mary cried out, I too cried out in my prayer time the next morning, *"These are leaders, Lord. Yet, they have taken prayer, Bible reading, the necessity of a daily quiet time and hearing personally from You away. As a result, You are nowhere to be found. Yes, they meet and serve in your name, but do they really KNOW You? I saw such little evidence."*

Prayer... Bible Reading... Listening for the direction of the Lord in their ministries did not appear to be part of the prevailing ethos for many of these leaders. Even when I asked, *"Did you pray about your spring*

CREATED FOR PURPOSE

event prior to the planning? Did you seek God's wisdom? What did He say?" Again, a church event and the response to these questions were women who looked at me like I had three heads. To their credit, they seemed genuinely interested in knowing more about what I was saying. This WAS encouraging.

Yet my heart mourned for the multitudes of women who rely on these shepherds[2] for spiritual guidance, but seemed to lack any real spiritual compass for themselves. I knew that unless something supernatural was happening, women en masse throughout my state were not coming to know Jesus personally. Yes, they may know Him as Savior, but not as Lord of their everyday lives. My heart grieved for all they may have been missing out on. After all, who was their role model for the Jesus Girl if their *"shepherd"* didn't even seem to truly know Him?

> Oswald Chambers says, *"The great enemy of the Lord Jesus Christ today is the idea of practical work… This work insists upon endless energy and activities, but no private life with God. The emphasis is on the wrong thing. The central point of the kingdom of Jesus Christ is a personal relationship with Him, not public usefulness to others."*[3]

4. Use verbs to describe what your private life with God look like:

_____

I grew up in church and have attended many different denominational churches in my adult life. Until recently, I have heard very few sermons on the importance of time spent cultivating a daily relationship with the God of the Universe. And sadly, to many in the Body of Christ, God is merely a *"Sunday morning God."*

All the while, we as a Body are busy serving, evangelizing, and sending people into foreign lands to build wells and to feed the hungry. Go into most any church and you will see evidence of this. All of which is really good! **I do not disagree with such work**, but my question is this:

> *How can we, as the Body of Christ, truly impact our corner of the world and share Him in a meaningful and impactful way, when in reality, we don't really know Him ourselves because of the shallowness of our private life with Him?*

REVELATION 2:1-5

5. List the ways Jesus commends the church of Ephesus in v2-3.

_____

_____

6. In what ways does the church at Ephesus remind you of the Church Girl?

_____

_____

7. However, what does Jesus say He holds against her? (v4) _____

8. What does Jesus encourage her to do? (v5a) _____

---

2   1 Peter 5:2-3
3   Oswald Chambers, *My Utmost for His Highest*; Discovery House Publishers, Grand Rapids, MI; Oct.19

WEEK 3 | DAY 2

9. What will result if she does not follow Jesus' directions? (v5b)

_____

_____

I love how encouraging the Lord is when we have inadvertently shifted from the path He desires us to be on. Allowing the Martha in us to dominate the Mary in us, He gently calls us to repentance and encourages us to do the things we did at first.

What were the things you did at first when you became a Christ follower? Has your work replaced your worship? Have activities replaced your own concentrated study time with the Lord? Have you allowed corporate settings to be your primary source of revelation instead of your own personal time with Him?

God is so sweet and faithful. He'll allow us to walk this path of busyness, but the warning is clear: if we do not return to Him, He takes away our *"lamp,"* meaning He takes away our effectiveness in ministry and in life. Our opportunities for living in the abundance and our *"light"* for others to see our Jesus will grow dim. Service is not enough; love for Jesus MUST come first.

PRIORITIES

10. What is to be our first priority? Mark 12:30.

_____

11. What is the second priority? Mark 12:31

_____

12. Following these two commandments is greater than what? Mark 12:33

_____

13. What are modern-day examples of burnt offerings and sacrifices? (We've discussed them all week)

_____

Let me say it again, so that I'm not misunderstood: It is extremely important to evangelize the lost, to go on mission trips, to feed the hungry and clothe the naked. And miraculously, God even uses our feeble attempts. But it's not the first commandment or priority according to Jesus.

Last week, I asked you to explain John 15:5. Let's look at the Amplified Translation:

> *"I am the Vine; you are the branches. Whoever lives in Me and I in him bears much (abundant) fruit. However, apart from Me [cut off from vital union with Me] you can do nothing."*

14. What does Jesus tell us is the prerequisite to a fruitful life in John 15:5?

_____

15. What can we do apart from vital union with Him? _____

16. How do John 15 and The Greatest Commandment correlate with each other?

_____

_____

I fell in love with my husband because I got to know him. I spent time with him, learning about his character. After 18 years of marriage, we still carve out quality time to reconnect. I know what makes him happy and I know what gets on his nerves. I know the kind of food he likes and the kind of food that gives him nothing to look forward to. It's my delight to serve him fresh put hair-on-your-chest kind of coffee each morning. It's my delight to make sure the lights are turned off when I leave a room and to make sure the bills are paid on time each month. These are things that are important to him, and I do them willingly because I love him and I know that these small things make him happy. I've taken time to KNOW him.

The same is true in our relationship with God. We cannot love someone or please someone whom we do not *truly* know. God wants for our knowledge of Him to be firsthand knowledge, not simply secondhand knowledge through a pastor, a friend, a Bible Study leader or a family member.

Also, notice that the Bible says to *"dwell in Him."* It does not say visit Him once a week and then ignore Him the rest of the time. The Bible says *"to abide in Him,"* not just call on Him when we get into trouble or find ourselves in desperate circumstances. The Bible says to be fruitful – it doesn't say be busy with endless activity. There's a difference between fruitfulness and busy activity.

Let me show you.

JOURNAL RESPONSE

Take a few moments to meditate on our study today.

Were there particular Scripture(s) or statement(s) that spoke to you personally?

1.

2.

3.

WEEK 3 | DAY 3

TODY'S TREASURE
...
"BUT SEEK FIRST HIS KINGDOM
AND HIS RIGHTEOUSNESS,
AND ALL THESE THINGS WILL
BE GIVEN TO YOU AS WELL."
MATTHEW 6:33

THE JESUS GIRL

1. What is the first step in coming to know and love Jesus firsthand? See Matthew 6:33

   _____

2. What happens when we make our relationship with Jesus the priority of our day? (John 15:5)

   _____

3. What will we be fruitful in? _____

When we seek Jesus first in daily priorities and abide in Him, we will be fruitful in whatever He tells us to do.[4]

Jesus was (and is) our perfect role model. Scripture tells us that He had a "certain place[5]" He went for prayer and fellowship with God. And when you read the gospels[6], prayer and time with God was how Jesus began His day. It was how He knew what to do and what not to do. It was how He knew when to go and when not to go.[7]

Please know this doesn't mean we quit serving Him in our corners of the world, but it does mean making our time with Jesus the first priority of the day. It does not mean being perfect, but it means pressing on.[8] It means putting Him first and arranging our schedules around Him. When we seek Him first and foremost, we can watch our lives fall into place.

4. What are hindrances do you face in spending quality time with Jesus each day?

   _____

5. How does Psalm 32:8 connect to Matthew 6:33? _____

   _____

---

[4] If this confuses you, worry not. We will address this concept in more detail in coming weeks.
[5] Luke 11:1
[6] The first 4 books of the New Testament: Matthew, Mark, Luke, and John
[7] Mark 1:35-39
[8] Philippians 3:12,14

One of the things that hinders me is my list of things to do. Another thing is my active mind. My to-do-list seems to scream once I sit in my quiet time space. HOWEVER, I deliberately push back the demands of these invisible voices in prayer by asking in Jesus' name that they be silenced. I then refuse to feel guilty about spending time sitting with Jesus – not in a hurry, but just savoring the peace that my soul so craves. As a result, amazing supernatural things begin to happen.

BENEFITS OF SPENDING TIME WITH JESUS

When the Bible says, *"I will instruct you and teach in the way you should go. I will guide you,"* it is true! Here are some of the benefits I have gleaned by seeking Jesus first and foremost:

- I seem to accomplish more in less time

- There's power for service out of my comfort zone (a power not my own, a power that can only come from Him.)

- My mind becomes aligned with His perspective so that I'm able to assimilate what IS important and what's NOT important for my day.

- I'm directed toward meaningful work, fruitful work.

- The negative thoughts that can plague me are silenced.

- The fearful thoughts that come from life's trials that seek to reappear and torment each day are silenced.

- I'm sweeter to my husband and gentler with my children. I have more patience.

- I have supernatural wisdom and insight for making decisions. I also have the confidence to stand firm with the decisions I've made – be it in parenting, in business, in ministry, etc.

6. What benefits have you gleaned from spending time with Him? _____

When we spend quality, regular time with God each day, we too will come to know Him personally. We too, will develop His heart and His mindset for our lives. Eventually, what breaks His heart will begin to break our hearts. He will reveal what His priorities are for our life.[9] We will know where to invest our time, our energy, our thoughts, our money, and our service. But most importantly, we'll come to know Him. And eventually, we'll come to love Him with all our heart, mind and soul.

7. How does Acts 17:28 connect to the Jesus Girl? (We saw this verse in Week 1)

_____

_____

---

9   Hebrews 12:1

JOURNAL RESPONSE

Take a few moments to meditate on our study today.

Were there particular Scripture(s) or statement(s) that spoke to you personally?

1.

2.

3.

WEEK 3 | DAY 4

TODAY'S TREASURE
...
"WHEN I CALLED [HER] SHE WAS BUT ONE, AND I BLESSED HER AND MADE HER MANY."
Isaiah 51:2

Church Girl to Jesus Girl

Years ago, one morning during my quiet time, I was reading *"A Wife After God's Own Heart."* Elizabeth George writes, *"If you do not have your husband's complete and total support in ministry, you must step out of service."* She goes on to say, *"Following God's will is that I follow my husband's leadership. This keeps me – and my service – in the center of God's will.* **No** *in an area of service can be God's will and direction as much as a yes can be."*[10]

I began coming out of Christian ministry to focus on my primary ministry at home. It was this book and the Scripture passages that opened my eyes to instinctively know the radical changes that needed to be made.

Would it be easy? NO. But it didn't matter. God was telling me through this little book and the accompanying Scriptures what God's will was for *"that season."*[11] So I grew some holy boldness, and withdrew from all areas of service. I finished my commitments or found replacements.

Yes, I was scared of disappointing my ministers and those who counted on me to fulfill my roles, but I was more afraid of not being in God's will. And I dreaded what could ultimately happen in my marriage if I continued the status quo.

As a result, peace returned to my home and my marriage. Not only that, but my husband responded more favorably to me because I had shown him respect by honoring his wishes without him even asking.

This was when I began making the transition from "Church girl" to "Jesus girl." I saw that Jesus' way worked. Sometimes it required sacrifice, but God was so sweet to allow me to see the fruit that would inevitably follow if I would be obedient in the small things as well as the big things. Before long, the Jesus Girl results became addictive. I had had a total paradigm shift and my life and family life became a place of extreme joy and peace. Not necessarily easy circumstances, but supernatural results from walking obediently with Jesus each day.

The Church Girl mentality does not go away easily – especially if you've been in the church for any length of time. There will always be a temptation for service to trump our personal time with the Lord. There will always be a temptation for philanthropic living or perfect attendance at prayer meetings to substitute for our time with Him.

---

10   *A Wife After God's Own Heart*, Elizabeth George. Harvest House Publishers; p189-191. 2004
11   There will be seasons that God calls says, "Go," and other times He says, "Stop." Spending time with Him and consistently listening to His voice is how we know when He's making changes in our seasons.

But in reality, these good things can be the greatest enemy if we are not careful, because all the good deeds in the world will not last for eternity unless you are doing one thing…

1. **And what is that one thing? (John 15:5)** _____

I hope you've memorized this verse by now! May we never forget, so that we can be about producing authentic fruit that impacts our corners of the world for Christ. It all starts with one woman.

ONE WOMAN

Authentic fruit… We've been talking about it for three weeks. What does it look like in everyday life? It will look differently for each one of us. But let me share common denominators of authentic fruit.

When one heart genuinely comes to the understanding that Jesus is real and falls in love with Him and begins living for Him and Him alone, a family changes. Marriages can be changed. Marriages can be healed.

The next generation will see that Jesus is real and that His commands in the Bible work in today's culture. Our children prayerfully begin to desire Him for themselves. Lifestyles of parents become worthy of imitating, and as a result, generations can possibly be forever changed due to the impact of one woman.

Why? **Because one woman grows some holy boldness.** One woman makes her time with God a priority and soon falls in love with Him. One woman's heart changes. And it soon impacts a family much like the power of a nuclear weapon – because God's Word and His blessings that fall on a radically obedient daughter are even more powerful than a weapon of this magnitude.

From there, communities, schools, the church, the workplace and our social circles can be transformed because our lifestyle backs up the fish on the back of our car or the cross around our neck. People take notice and want to KNOW our God. They want to understand our supernatural peace when faced with the harshest of hardships. They want to know why we have supernatural joy in the midst of crummy life circumstances.

Why? Because one woman becomes intentional in her relationship with God. She begins to see firsthand that this *"Jesus stuff"* works in everyday life. He's no longer a *"Sunday morning God"* or a name in a ritual to be practiced, but a God that is personal and will be closer than the closest friend. This one woman soon becomes much like Peter and John in Acts 4:20.

2. **What is happening in Acts 4:20?**

_____

I see something organic happening in this passage. And I too can identify with it. When we begin to see results from obedience spurred by our time with God, the praises and testimonies about what Jesus does in our everyday lives will roll off our tongues with ease. We will not be able to help but speak about what we have seen and heard Jesus do in response to prayer or obedience to His Word!

The testimonies you have read and will continue to read in this Bible Study are me sharing with you – what I have seen and heard as a result of ME being intentional in my relationship with Jesus and choosing to follow hard after Him. When I say that He will take our lives and allow us to live in ways that are bigger than ourselves, I mean it! I've watched Him do it with others around me, and I'm watching Him do it in me!

WEEK 3 | DAY 4

3. **In what ways can you publicly testify to your Bible study group or to a friend about what you have seen Jesus do in your everyday life as a result of answered prayer or obedience to His Word?**

_____

_____

WHERE MINISTRY STARTS

If you are married, ministry starts in the home, especially if you have children. If you are not married, ministry is where you are in life. Ministry is where you work; it's in the stores you frequent or the coffee shop you visit. It's with your immediate family and circle of friends. It's in your hobbies. And it's in the church. THIS is where ministry starts.

You see, bearing fruit does not necessarily mean moving to Africa and living in hut. (Though HE does call people to do this – but when He does, He gives us the passion and power and for this mission and purpose.) But even for the woman called to live in an African hut, ministry would start within the walls of her hut. Fruitful living starts in our homes – within our families… Starting with:

#1: Our relationship with God. Our relationship with God is the most important thing in our lives. Our relationship cannot be based on what we do for God. It's based on our private life with Him.

#2: Our spouse. Our first, primary ministry is to our husband[12] – not to everyone else and then him. And don't forget, apart from a vibrant relationship with Jesus, we cannot be a good spouse.

#3: Our children. Loving and caring for them. Educating them, clothing them and feeding them; Being their taxi to all their extracurricular activities. But the most important thing we do for our children is to teach them to love the Lord Jesus for themselves.[13] Their education and their sports commitments are secondary.

#4: Our homes. Our homes should be a peaceful sanctuary[14]. We can make our homes a slice of heaven here on earth by creating an inviting atmosphere, an atmosphere that is peaceful, loving and positive, a place that everyone looks forward to coming home to. Pray through the rooms of your home; keep it clean and orderly; keep food on hand that your husband and everyone else loves.

#5: Our Families – our parents and extended family. God has called us to honor our parents.[15] I realize that to the woman who has parents she does not feel are worthy of honor, this may be difficult. However, it is still a command in God's Word. So the way you may honor your parents may look different from the way I honor my parents.[16] We make time for them in our lives either by phone calls or visiting. When they grow old and need help, we are not to ignore them by turning them over to a care facility to look after while we continue our lives as though they were invisible. Yes, we may move our elderly parents into a care facility, but if we do, we must also visit and continue to love them and serve them. We take them to doctor's appointments or just be there for them. This is honoring God.

#6: Our Jobs outside the home. Anything outside the home is a mission field in and of itself.

#7: Our Ministries in the church, in our communities, schools, in foreign lands etc…

#8: Our friends.

---

12 Genesis 2:18; Titus 2:4
13 Deuteronomy 6:5-9; Joshua 8:35
14 Proverbs 31:27; Proverbs 14:1
15 Exodus 20:12 Ten Commandments; Matthew 19:19
16 Appropriate boundaries can be made. If you need help with appropriate boundaries, see your Pastor or a Christian Counselor.

ARE YOU WILLING?

4. **Are you willing to be that** *"one woman"*? _____

Read Today's Treasure and then let's apply it to our "One Woman."

5. **When** *"One Woman"* **determines to say yes to God and to follow hard after Him, what does God promise to do?** _____

May we never forget, apart from a vibrant relationship with Jesus, our parenting or grandparenting will be fruitless. Apart from a vibrant relationship with Jesus, our work, our hobbies, our church or philanthropic service WILL BE FRUITLESS in the eyes of the Gardener.

And though our work may look like fruit – Jesus is the Vine. He's the One Who determines if it's fruit or merely the appearance of fruit.

It's all about the heart… Our bodies can be in our churches and our hearts can be sincere, but apart from Him, we can do *nothing* of eternal significance. Don't be fooled.

JOURNAL RESPONSE

Take a few moments to meditate on our study today.

Were there particular Scripture(s) or statement(s) that spoke to you personally?

1.

2.

3.

REVIEW

1. What were the most meaningful or significant lessons you learned each day?

   Day 1: _____
   _____

   Day 2: _____
   _____

   Day 3: _____
   _____

   Day 4: _____
   _____

2. Is there anything you sense God telling you to do as a result of the study this week? If so, share.
   _____
   _____

3. What action steps do you need to take in order to be obedient?
   _____
   _____

4

SHIFTS OF THE HEART

WEEK FOUR

Day 1 | A Paradigm Shift in the Heart

Day 2 | Waking our Hearts

Day 3 | The Secret Places of the Heart

Day 4 | The Secret Attitudes of the Heart

Day 5 | Review

WEEK 4 | DAY 1

TODAY'S TREASURE
...
"IN THE YEAR THAT KING UZZIAH
DIED, I SAW THE LORD."
ISAIAH 6:1

A Paradigm Shift in the Heart

A paradigm shift can be defined as *"a change from one way of thinking to another.¹"* So it is my prayer that in the last two weeks, we've experienced a paradigm shift in three different areas of our thinking.

Let's review:

Paradigm Shift #1: What matters in life and what doesn't.

Paradigm Shift #2: The realization of the Church girl and the Jesus girl.

Paradigm Shift #3: Time spent serving the Lord is not the same as time spent with Him.

1. **In your own words, summarize the difference between the Church girl and the Jesus girl.**

   _____
   _____

2. **What did Jesus say about serving Him vs. time spent with Him? (John 15:5)**

   _____

May we never forget that apart from spending meaningful time with Jesus, in His Word and in prayer, we can do nothing of lasting value. Our lives will have little purpose or meaning in the eyes of He who counts – the One to whom we must answer. God loves us so much and desires to enlarge our lives. He desires for our lives to be fruitful, significant and meaningful in our corners of the world. However, many of us need a wake-up call, whether we realize it or not.

ISAIAH'S WAKE-UP CALL

This week, we will turn our focus to Isaiah. It is said that Isaiah is the most outstanding of all the Old Testament prophets, yet the start of his ministry did not indicate his God-ordained significance. In fact, from my personal study, it would seem that his relationship with God was very legalistic.

Record **phrases** of how God communicated to Isaiah. I'll give you the first one.

3. **Isaiah 1:10:** *"Hear the Word of the Lord..."*

1

CREATED FOR PURPOSE

4. Isaiah 1:24 _____

_____

5. Isaiah 2:1 _____

_____

6. Isaiah 3:16 _____

_____

7. Isaiah 5:9 _____

_____

8. What do you notice about Isaiah's relationship with God?
_____

As you evaluate the tone of Isaiah and God's relationship, keep in mind, Isaiah was God's chosen vessel during this particular time in history. As we've learned, you and I have been strategically placed[2] in ***this*** generation during ***this*** period in history. From the moment we invite the Lord Jesus into our lives, we too become God's chosen vessels.[3]

Now notice the tone of the relationship *following his paradigm shift in Isaiah 6:1-7*. Write the phrases:

9. Isaiah 7:3 _____ *"Then the Lord said to Isaiah…"*

10. Isaiah 8:1 _____

_____

11. Isaiah 8:5 _____

_____

12. Isaiah 8:11 _____

_____

13. What do you notice about Isaiah's relationship with God now?
_____

It would be *one incident… one event* that would catapult one man into a personal, dynamic relationship with his God. He would be forever different, forever changed. And there would be no going back. From this event, he would rise to become the man God had always intended him to be. He would live with such great significance that his work and insight for God's people would be forever recorded in the canon of Scripture. What was this event that caused Isaiah's paradigm shift?

---

2   Acts 17:26
3   Timothy 2:21

WEEK 4 | DAY 1

QUICK HISTORY LESSON

It's worth noting that 739 BC[4] was approximately the year that the city of Rome was in founded, and subsequently, the Roman Empire. And it's also interesting to see that while the Bible makes no mention of such a momentous event in the world, it does devote an entire chapter to describing one man's experience of personal revival. The conclusion is that one person waking up in his relationship with God, is more important, from God's perspective, than an entire world empire being established.[5]

THE THRONE ROOM

Read Isaiah 6:1 and answer the following questions.

14. What was this difficult event for Isaiah? _____

15. As a result of this incident, what happened? (v1a _____

16. What do you think this means in practical terms? _____

In the year that King Uzziah died… In the year of great heartache… In the year of great hardship… Isaiah saw the Lord! He had a fresh encounter with the Living God of the Universe that would forever change the way He served Him and the way he approached Him.

17. What did Isaiah see during this fresh encounter? (Summarize v2-5)

_____

_____

18. Who was it that Isaiah saw? _____

Isaiah saw God sitting on His throne in the fullness of His glory. Isaiah's eyes were opened afresh and it would forever change him. John records this in his gospel, *"Isaiah saw Jesus' glory and spoke about Him."* John 12:41. The glory Isaiah saw was Jesus Christ Himself.

19. I'd like for you to read two other similar revelations of Jesus' glory: Ezekiel 1:22-28 and Revelation 4: 1-6. From each passage, record the basic similarities and additional descriptions.

Ezekiel 1: 22-28 - _____

_____

_____

Revelation 4: 1-6 - _____

_____

_____

---

4   http://www.dailymail.co.uk/news/article-2312567/When-Rome-The-Eternal-City-takes-step-time-celebrates-2-766th-birthday.html
5   Anne Graham Lotz, *Expecting to SEE Jesus*; Zondervan 2011; pp.90-91

20. What is your heart's response to these passages of Scripture? Is this new to you?

_____

_____

Sweet friend, do you and I have any idea whom we approach when bow to our knees in prayer, or bow our head in a restaurant or wherever we may pray? Can our finite minds truly comprehend the wonder, the majesty, the holiness and splendor of God Almighty? That He loves us so much that He made a way for us to approach the very throne room of grace 24 hours a day/7 days a week because of the blood shed for us by His precious Son, Jesus? AND that He's glad to see us when we come to Him in prayer?![6]

To me, it's mind-blowing that God Himself in all His power, glory, majesty and splendor, allows us to see Jesus enthroned. This same God desires us to know Him intimately and personally on the anvil of everyday life. God wants us to live and move and find our being in Him. He wants for our eyes to be opened, just as Isaiah's eyes were, to a fresh revelation of glory that catapulted him out of spiritual complacency so that he was no longer indifferent to God and His people and no longer merely *"going through the motions"* of religion.

But let's not forget what it took to awaken Isaiah: hardship and heartache.

JOURNAL RESPONSE

Take a few moments to meditate on our study today.

Were there particular Scripture(s) or statement(s) that spoke to you personally?

1.

2.

3.

---

6   Ephesians 3:12 NLT

WEEK 4 | DAY 2

TODAY'S TREASURE

...

"THE LORD SPOKE TO ME..."
ISAIAH 8:11, (MY ITALICS)

Waking our Hearts

Yesterday, we were eyewitnesses to Isaiah's wake-up call. Please understand, the Bible does not indicate prior to Isaiah's fresh vision of the Lord that thought he was in need of a wake-up call or paradigm shift from God. Isaiah thought he was spiritually just fine. From his point of view, he was doing all the right things. If we aren't careful, we too can feel the same way.

1. **Connecting what we studied last week when Jesus spoke to the church of Sardis in Revelation 3:2, what was happening to Isaiah? Fill in the blanks: Isaiah was _____!**

It thrills the enemy for us to serve God tirelessly, yet be spiritually complacent or indifferent. This is right where Satan desires us to be. Yet, when we make meaningful, simple prayer, Bible reading and obedience to God a priority, he trembles. Why? Because this is when we become a threat to the powers of darkness. This is when we begin to live our God-ordained purpose.

QUICK HISTORY LESSON

King Uzziah's death was a time of great difficulty and distress for Isaiah. Why? According to tradition, there is a slight chance that King Uzziah was a relative of Isaiah's. Also, Isaiah's burden may have been heavier because of the knowledge that Uzziah, as he had grown older, had allowed pride to rule his life until he was no longer pleasing to God. Isaiah's grief may have been intensified knowing that his loved one died while being separated from God. And then there's the thought of finances. It is said that Isaiah lived in the palace. His needs were probably very generously met. He never worried about where his next meal was coming from or affordable housing or how he would pay his child's tuition for school, etc. In fact, he may never have had to budget at all. But now the king was dead, and the possibility exists that Isaiah's cash flow was suddenly cut-off, shaking him financially in addition to everything else he had to endure.[7]

Sadly, it may have taken something this painful to finally get Isaiah's attention.

GOD USES HARDSHIPS TODAY

God uses hardships and difficulties to wake us as well. He'll allow hardships to come into our lives as a way of getting our attention; to shake us emotionally and spiritually. Why does He do this? Because He desires for us to **wake up**. He wants to give us a fresh vision that forever changes the way we view Him and forever changes the way we view church. God wants for Jesus to become <u>real</u> in our everyday lives, so that we no longer try to pigeonhole Him as a "Sunday morning habit" or think of him primarily in terms of a building that we visit once a week.

---

[7] Anne Graham Lotz, *Expecting to SEE Jesus*; Zondervan 2011; p91-94

CREATED FOR PURPOSE

2. What hardship are you currently facing? (Or have you recently faced?)

_____

3. How could God be using this hardship to get your attention?

_____

MY FIRST WAKE-UP CALL

Ten years after the fact, I praise God that He allowed my marriage to start falling apart at the seams. Up until then, I was big-time church girl, yet God was not real to me. He was a Sunday morning habit and the God of antiquity – certainly not of the twenty-first century!

Yet one day, I reached my pressure point, the point where I could not stand it anymore. This forced me[8] to seek God's ways. Nothing else had worked. I had tried everything from asking my friends for their advice to even emulating the actions of my friends – especially if they seemed to be getting results in their marriages. This did not work for me. In fact, it made my situation worse.

Let's pause for a moment and talk about your *pressure point*. The pressure point can be described as the point in our circumstances when we are at our maximum capacity and can take no more.

4. Have you ever reached your pressure point? _____ How do you respond when this happens?

_____

In January 2003, my pressure point was boiling over. Exasperated and angry, I went to my knees following an argument with my husband. It was over the same subject we had argued about for years. My face was in the carpet… Tears were streaming down my cheeks… I begged God to change my husband and to change my marriage.

Suddenly, I received my answer.

The answer I received was, frankly, not one that I expected or liked. In fact, I thought God had it all wrong. Yet the answer would catapult me out of my complacent, legalistic, rote relationship with Jesus. In the year that I thought I could take no more, God told me that the change in my marriage would not start with my husband. Instead, change would start with *me*.[9] Though I did not like this answer, nor did I agree with God, I was desperate and willing to try anything.

That particular week, we were studying John 12. Death to self was the big lesson. God seemed to be telling me from my Bible study, that if I wanted life to come back into my marriage,[10] than I would have die to having to have the last word; die to always having to have my way; die to having to be in control.

The following week, John 13 was about service – starting with the people in my home by doing the lowliest task around the house. During this same period of time, a mentor gave me the book, The Politically

---
8   Sadly at the time, going to God to meet my everyday needs was my last resort, not my first response.
9   This is when I became "One Woman": when I embraced the change.
10 2 Corinthians 4:12

Incorrect Wife.[11] This book amazingly corresponded to what I was learning in my Bible study. This was not a coincidence. This was God Almighty Himself, reaching down from His Throne room in heaven and answering the desperate cry of one woman... and by so doing, giving me a fresh vision of Himself by revealing to me very practically, the changes I needed to make in order for *life* to come back into my marriage. As a result, my eyes were opened for the first time – much as Isaiah's were, to a fresh vision of the Lord.

Did I visibly see Him?

No. But I **saw** that as **I applied** what I was learning in my quiet time and Bible study to my marriage, **CHANGE HAPPENED! Jesus way's worked!** I experienced firsthand behind the doors of my home that Jesus is not just a building I went to once a week, nor is He the social hour for moral living with a bunch of girls that we sometimes call *"Bible Study,"* because we leave that study without allowing the Word to impact everyday life choices. Jesus is REAL, and His ways and methods as outlined in the Bible actually work! His Word is true and successfully operates in the twenty-first century despite what the world around us says. It's the ancient path, and it works! This began my paradigm shift from *"Sister Super Christian"* to *"Jesus girl."*

Now to people on the outside, it looked like I was forsaking God because I was pulling out of many areas of Christian service that I had formerly been involved with. Yet I was exactly where God wanted me to be – attending to my primary ministry: the people within my home, starting with my husband.

Personally for me, my paradigm shift centered around the realization that God speaks! Moreover, He'll speak to the everyday people like me and you in our everyday problems, dilemmas and hard aches... I have not been the same since that realization! And as of this writing, it's been over 10 years.

5. **If you are in a trial or hardship of any kind... (Be honest)**

   a. Have you spent time in personal prayer?   Yes   or   No

   b. Have you sought what the Lord has to say about your trial?   Yes   or   No

   c. Have you followed up with meaningful obedience?   Yes   or   No

It's okay if the answer is not a yes to all of these questions. By the end of this study, you'll be ready to give a resounding YES to all of those questions. Oh, the blessings we miss when we fail to follow up with meaningful obedience!

6. **Today I shared my story of when Jesus became real to me. Has Jesus become REAL to you? Please note, this is most likely not when you became a believer. As it was with Isaiah, it may be a separate experience altogether. If you've had such an experience, share it with your group.**

_____

_____

---

11 *The Politically Incorrect Wife*, Nancy Cobb and Connie Grigsby; Multnomah Books; 2000; a personal favorite I highly recommend.

"The Lord spoke to Isaiah…" With confidence I can say that throughout the pages of my prayer journal, I have recorded what *"the Lord has said to Tara…"* Those words are what sustain me each day, but especially in the year that great hardships fall.

If Jesus has not become real to you, do not be embarrassed. But get ready, girlfriend. May this be the year that, *"The Lord spoke to _____."* (Insert your name.)

JOURNAL RESPONSE

Take a few moments to meditate on our study today.

Were there particular Scripture(s) or statement(s) that spoke to you personally?

1.

2.

3.

WEEK 4 | DAY 3

TODAY'S TREASURE
...
"THE DAY IS COMING WHEN GOD, THROUGH CHRIST JESUS, WILL JUDGE EVERYONE'S SECRET LIFE."
ROMANS 2: 16 NLT

THE SECRET PLACES OF THE HEART

I don't know about you, but I would describe the world we live in today as being in total denial: Total denial that there are consequences to bad behavior. Culture tells us we can sleep with whomever, whenever, and there will be no consequences. That we should do whatever feels good or whatever feels right and to heck with the consequences. That we can have an entirely different life if we choose… Perhaps a virtual secret life or a secret life that either involves our minds, emotions and at times, our bodies. It could be a physical affair, or an emotional affair. It could be flirting with an old flame on Facebook. No one sees. No one knows…

Or so it would seem.

And then there's anger, resentfulness, bitterness and unforgiveness towards others. You can't always see any of these things with the naked eye, but they're there. And often instead of dealing with these issues, we tend to coddle, nurture, or excuse them. However, God in His great love commands us to deal with the secret junk in our lives, otherwise known as: our stuff!

1. **From Today's Treasure, how does Scripture contradict the mentality of** *"no consequences"*?

   _____

But *"A day is coming…"* when we WILL face the Judge. We studied this firsthand in Week 2 and we saw firsthand that there will be consequences! We may not visibly see any consequences NOW for immoral, unethical or wrong behavior, however, *the day* is coming when not only everyone's visible life, but their secret life, will be judged as well.

When Isaiah's eyes were opened afresh in His relationship with God, he saw God's holiness and purity. Suddenly, something immediately sent shock waves through his soul. It terrified Isaiah. It made him deeply embarrassed and ashamed.

2. **Read Isaiah 6:4-5. What was it that made him ashamed before the Lord?**

   _____

Before we can see the Lord afresh, we must see sin for what it is – blatant or hidden. We cannot excuse it or make excuses for it. We cannot turn a blind eye and condone it or even coddle it. We must acknowledge its presence in our life and deal with it, even in the secret places of our heart.

Let's not be in denial with the rest of the world: God sees the heart, whether we want Him to or not.

3. How does Psalm 90:8 reiterate that we can hide NOTHING from God? (Write out the passage)

_____

_____

Today's study may be difficult and raw for some of you. Yet it is vitally important if we want to progress in obtaining all that God desires to give us. This will require us allowing the Lord to search the deep, secret places of our heart. It will require gut-level honesty with God. Yet please know, it's what unlocks the floodgates for a fresh encounter with the Lord Jesus.

4. Before we go any further, bow your head in prayer and give the Lord permission to shine the light of His Presence into the recesses of your heart, into the secret places that no one sees.

   O _____ Check the circle when you have prayed.

So that you may be encouraged before we begin this exercise, let's jump ahead to what happened following Isaiah's confession and repentance.

5. Read Isaiah 6:7-9. What did this prepare Isaiah for? _____

His confession prepared him to serve God in a meaningful and significant way in his corner of the world. Orders straight from the throne room of heaven started Isaiah on the path marked for him.[12] Awareness of sin in our lives, confession and repentance are vital components to living a life of significance in our corner of the world. I'll share first.

GOD'S INTERRUPTION

I vividly remember having such an awareness of God's awareness of my secret sin, that I literally looked in the backseat of my car to see if anyone was sitting there. I worked for Bausch and Lomb and was traveling on Interstate 64 near Virginia Beach and the Chesapeake Bay area. I was between doctor calls.

On my way to the next appointment, I began indulging my thought life and began to think about not very good things. (Keep in mind, I was a Bible study leader and Sunday School teacher at the time.) And my thoughts – though entertaining, were NOT holy.

That day, I did not hear an audible voice – but it sure sounded like it in my heart. The voice was clear and specific: *"If you want to really know Me and if you want promotion, these thoughts have to go. NO MORE."*

Like Isaiah, when I became keenly aware that my thoughts were not pleasing to God, I repented that very moment. I acknowledged that these thoughts were NOT thoughts God wanted me to have, and I asked Him for strength to turn away from them.

SECRET LIFE AND PROMOTION

What are your dreams? What are the desires of your heart? We all have them. For ease of explanation, I'll call the dreams and desires of our heart "promotion."

---
12 Hebrews 12:1

WEEK 4 | DAY 3

6. How does Psalm 37:4 connect our secret thought life and promotion? _____

_____

Please know that promotion as used here is not necessarily referring to a work situation or a higher salary. I'm referring to kingdom promotion: In other words, the life God desires for us to have; for our life to matter outside of our lifetime. Promotion means having the desires of our heart met; desires for the fruitful life, the abundant life, the life of immense blessing.

More than anything, I want promotion!

7. What is the pre-requisite to promotion according to Psalm 37:4a? _____

8. What do you think this phrase means? _____

_____

Holiness and sin CANNOT co-habitate. My secret thoughts… thoughts that were not good; thoughts that were not holy – HAD TO GO. The same goes for you. If you and I want the desire of our hearts met, known sin in all forms, shapes and sizes must go. We must be flexible and moldable for God by listening to Him and responding to His Word whether we like the Word or not.

Read Psalm 66:17-19

9. When we choose to hold onto our sin, what does God call this? _____

10. What is the result? _____

11. When we do not cherish sin, what is promised? (v19) _____

_____

Do you see the connection of our "secret life" to promotion and the life of significance in God's eyes? Our secret life is not a separate entity. And if we desire for our prayers to be heard; for God in His throne room to listen to us when we plea before the throne of mercy for help, we need to let go of the sins we may be cherishing in our heart.

My friend Cindy calls these sins our "pets." By that she means that we really like and enjoy some sins, making it hard to let them go. Thoughts of bitterness, unforgiveness, anger, worry, resentfulness, criticism, judgmentalism, superiority, racism, or pornography – anything that is not holy and pure – must go!

12. You don't have to answer out loud if you don't want to. You may even want to write in code. What has God brought to mind as you've read today: _____

_____

If we truly want our lives to matter outside of our lifetime, EVERYTHING must be on the table: The good, the bad, and the ugly. God's a Big God. He can deal with it. Don't hold back. He already knows.

Prepare your heart for repentance.

JOURNAL RESPONSE

Take a few moments to meditate on our study today.

Were there particular Scripture(s) or statement(s) that spoke to you personally?

1.

2.

3.

WEEK 4 | DAY 4

TODAY'S TREASURE
...
"THE SACRIFICES OF GOD ARE A BROKEN SPIRIT AND CONTRITE HEART, O GOD, YOU WILL NOT DESPISE."
PSALM 51:17

THE SECRET ATTITUDES OF THE HEART

Praise God that our past does not preclude us from being used by God in mighty, extraordinary ways! However, indulgence or cherishing known sin in the secret places of the heart will most certainly not only have consequences but WILL disqualify us from having ALL THE LORD WANTS TO GIVE US.

Before we can fully repent from what God may have revealed yesterday, I want to examine our heart attitude toward God and our time with Him. These secret attitudes lurk deep. We may not even be aware they exist – or perhaps we are aware of them. Confronting the secret attitudes of the heart is vital to moving forward.

As we begin, let me ask you a few personal questions… Be honest with yourself.

1. **Do you really want to hear what the God of the Universe desires to say to you and your circumstances?**

   _____

Sometimes, we really don't want to hear what He has to say because we are afraid of change or what He might say to us. We may not want to change an area of our lifestyles. We may be willing to change every area – but not ONE certain area.

2. **What if read something in your Bible that you'd rather not hear. How does your heart respond?**

   _____

It's easy to ignore or to rationalize a direction away to mean something else by having the *"surely this passage is not talking about me"* attitude. When God says, *"Submit to your husband,"* what is your immediate reaction? Do you tense up and explain that certainly this is not meant for modern women?

3. **What if it requires lifestyle change, how does your heart respond? Are you willing?**

   _____

"Surely God isn't telling me to do that," you may say to yourself. To follow scripture might cause embarrassment, you fear, and *"I don't want to be labeled a radical."*

CREATED FOR PURPOSE

THE HEART

The years that my quiet time with God was rote and legalistic were also a time when my heart was not *quite right* before the Lord. Yes, I had acknowledged the secret sins of my heart and had repented. But there was something else. Perhaps you too can relate.

Deep down, in the inner recesses of my heart, I genuinely wanted to hear from God… BUT… if it required too much of a change in my lifestyle… No thank you! I was not interested. OR if it required letting go of an area of my lifestyle that I highly valued… No thank you! I'd want to turn to another page and read about God's love for me! (Talk about selective listening…)

Read Isaiah 66:2

4. What two things does the Lord esteem? _____
   _____

5. What does this mean to you? _____
   _____

I don't mean for this to be in any way condemning. I'm merely sharing a known reality. In the Body of Christ, we see:

> Divorce rates skyrocketing;
>> Believers who are sexually active outside of marriage;
> Believers addicted to pornography and other strongholds or what we may refer to as vices;
>> Believers who are married and flirting on Facebook, at work conferences, at church, etc.;
>>> Believers who are angry; bitter; living in unforgiveness;
>> Believers with a complete and total disregard for their in-laws;
>>> Believers with a total disregard for their own mothers and fathers.

So, how do you respond when in your quiet time, God impresses something on your heart that you don't want to hear? Do you tremble at the Word of the Lord? Or do you disregard it, thinking, *"He can't be talking about that. Surely, He's not telling me to…"*

I've had Him reveal areas of pride and unforgiveness in my life. I've had Him impress upon my heart to apologize, even when it would be humiliatingly embarrassing to do so… even when what I apologized for was not my fault.

REPENTANCE

6. In Isaiah 6:5, what is taking place in Isaiah? _____

7. Following Isaiah's awareness and repentance of his sin, (v6-7)

   a. a. What was taken from the altar?
      _____

   b. b. Who took it from the altar?
      _____

WEEK 4 | DAY 4

    c. c. What did it do? (7c)

_____

Just as Isaiah became aware, confessed and repented, God used a seraph (an angel) to retrieve a burning coal from the altar. The application of the coal was enough to not only atone for Isaiah's sin, but to *remove the guilt as well*.

8. Today, this side of the cross of Christ, in lieu of a burning coal, how do we do to have our sin forgiven? (See 1 John 1:9)

    a. a. What is our part?

_____

    b. b. What is Jesus' part?

_____

Jesus did the same for us when He willingly laid down His life on the cross. Jesus' death on the cross represents the seraph, and the coal represents His blood, that was shed for you and for me.[13] Jesus' blood not only atones for our sin[14], but also removes the guilt associated with our sin. Glory to God!

BUSINESS WITH GOD

What is God bringing to mind today? Whatever is holding you back from having a humble and contrite spirit – whatever is holding you back from trembling at His Word, bring it to Him. Tell Him you're having a hard time letting this go. Tell Him you want to let it go…

- Could it be a grudge you are holding against your mother-in-law or even your own mother? Repent.

- Is it a grudge against your husband or a friend? Forgive and repent.

- Is it anger, bitterness or resentfulness toward another? Forgive and repent.

- Could it be a sexual desire for another man other than your husband?[15] Repent.

- Could it be flirting on Facebook with another man or past boyfriend? Burn the bridge and repent!

- Is it a constant critical or complaining spirit? Repent and begin THANKING GOD for what you have.

- Is it constant worry? Repent and begin TRUSTING!

- Is it taking God's Word too lightly? Not revering His Word? Confess this to Him and begin revering His Word.

- Is it an addiction? A destructive relationship? – End it; Repent and begin a new start.

---

13   See Hebrews 7:27; 10:19-22
14   Hebrews 9:12, 28
15   Matthew 5:27-30

CREATED FOR PURPOSE

- Is it not willing to make lifestyle adjustments based on what God is showing you? – Obey and prepare to be blessed!

(By the way, when we hold on to unforgiveness towards someone, we're only hurting ourselves. Unforgiveness keeps us in bondage. Release any such person to Jesus and allow Him to deal with them.[16] His way of dealing with them will be far more effective than your way of dealing with them. Not to mention, it's a prerequisite for having our own sins forgiven, as the Lord's Prayer makes clear.)

Let's do business with God by emulating Isaiah's example:

1. Acknowledge before the Lord what the sin is. Name it.

2. Confess whatever the Lord has brought to mind over the last few days.

3. Tell God that you desire to Repent. Repentance means to turn back to God…

Frances Chan, in Forgotten God,[17] writes a beautiful prayer of repentance, *"Sweet Jesus, You are the best thing that has ever happened to me! I want to turn from all the sin and selfishness that rules me. I want to let it go and walk with You. Only You. You are my life now. Help me to walk away from the enslaving, worthless things in my life."*

9. From Psalm 51:17, what are the sacrifices of God? The sacrifices that HE will not despise?

_____

Broken and contrite, will you ask God now to nail what He has put on your heart to the cross? Name the sin… Do not excuse it or rename it by giving it a friendlier name or a pet name… If you make light of your sin or excuse it, you are only robbing yourself of the rich blessings that are waiting for you.

There is no sin that is too big for our loving and merciful God. However, repentance also includes making sure that we forgive ourselves. If we fail to forgive ourselves, we put ourselves in the place of God by, in essence, telling Him that what we think is more important than what He thinks. Be careful in this area. Memorize the healing, redemptive words of Romans 8:1, *"There is NOW no condemnation for those who are in Christ Jesus."* This is truth that we can stand firm upon. Let the bones that God crushed at the revelation of these secret sinful places in the heart, rejoice! (Psalm 51:8)

10. Following repentance, what are great phrases to pray for ourselves from Psalm 51:10-12?

_____

_____

Living significant lives in our corners of the world requires hard, ongoing work. Please know that it is an ongoing job to turn from old familiar habits and pet sins to embrace the life God has for us. We will never be perfect this side of heaven, but we continue to press on. Keeping a clear conscience as best we know by maintaining a pure heart is where we are called to start each day. God is faithful. Our labor to have pure hearts WILL be rewarded.

I love the old hymn, *"It is Well with My Soul."* My favorite verse says,

---

16 16 Matthew 5:23-26; 6:14-15
17 Frances Chan, (Colorado Springs, CO:David Cook Publishing; 2009), 124

WEEK 4 | DAY 4

"My sin, not in part, but the whole…
Is nailed to the Cross and I bear it no more.
Praise the Lord, Praise the Lord, oh my soul."

Begin to bask in His Presence, dear one. When we hold nothing back – He in turn will hold nothing back. You have prepared yourself for a fresh encounter that will catapult you into all God desires to give you!

JOURNAL RESPONSE

Take a few moments to meditate on our study today.

Were there particular Scripture(s) or statement(s) that spoke to you personally?

1.

2.

3.

CREATED FOR PURPOSE

WEEK 4 | DAY 5

REVIEW

1. What were the most meaningful or significant lessons you learned each day?

   Day 1: _____

   _____

   Day 2: _____

   _____

   Day 3: _____

   _____

   Day 4: _____

   _____

2. Is there anything you sense God telling you to do as a result of the study this week? If so, share.

   _____

   _____

3. What action steps do you need to take in order to be obedient?

   _____

   _____

5

LISTENING FOR PURPOSE

WEEK FIVE

Day 1 | You Were Created to Hear from God

Day 2 | The Soil of our Heart

Day 3 | Hearing from God Personally

Day 4 | How to Hear His Voice

Day 5 | Review

TODAY'S TREASURE

...

"HE WHO BELONGS TO GOD HEARS WHAT GOD SAYS."
John 8:47

YOU WERE CREATED TO HEAR FROM GOD

I realize the last few weeks may have been really hard. Please know that you are not alone. But living the life of abundan[ce] and purpose will not be easy work. Some of us will have to work harder than others as we give Jesus unhindered access to [our] hearts and minds. But the rewards are worth it, sweet sister. Persevere. I can testify to the good that comes from continua[lly] giving the Lord unhindered access into the places of my heart and mind. I promise you that He never uses it to bring shame or embarrassment, but He uses it to bring us freedom and wholeness![1]

Last week I asked the question: **Do you believe that God will to speak to you?**

YOU! The one who perhaps has worn a Scarlet Letter?
    YOU, the one who may have limited Bible knowledge?
        YOU, the one who was not raised going to church?
            YOU, the one who has major life issues and struggles?
                YOU, the one who feels so unworthy?

Whenever I used to hear people say, *"The Lord told me to…,"* I thought they were weird! *"How could anyone hear the L[ord] speak"* I'd ask myself. However, the more I understand Scripture, the more I understand how personal and intimate G[od] desires to be with His creation. Now, I can't live without His tender, sweet voice – especially during seasons of difficu[lty] and hardship.

1. **What are your thoughts on the subject of God speaking personally to you? Is this a new thought?**

   _____

2. **What is your previous exposure to this concept?**

   _____

3. **How does Jesus' statement in Scripture reiterate the fact that we were created to hear from God? (John 8:47 Today's Treasure)**

   _____

Oh, how I wish I could hear your answers! This subject has become the passion of my life! To me it's profound that t[he] God of the Universe would speak personally to me and to you. That He'll speak about major life issues as well as mi[nor] life issues. I'm addicted to my time with God. And when trials and tribulations come… When there are decisions to mak[e]

---

[1] Isaiah 61:1-3

CREATED FOR PURPOSE

When I receive bad news… The *only person* I want to hear from is my Jesus. And until I hear personally from Him, I'd prefer not to hear anyone else's opinion or thoughts. Often their voices tend to only confuse me, making me indecisive.

PRECONCEIVED IDEAS

I used to think that God only spoke to the important people of the world – like the Billy Grahams, the Beth Moores, the preachers and teachers. Certainly, ordinary people like me could never know Him the way the greats of the Bible and the greats of my generation know Him. And certainly, I thought, people with a past like mine are never worthy enough to hear His voice.

4. **What preconceived ideas about God speaking have you entertained?**
   _____

5. **Read Isaiah 45:19 NLT and answer the following questions.**

"I would not have told the people of Israel to seek Me if I could not be found."

   a. **Who are the New Testament "people of Israel?"** _____

   b. **Who is the "Me" in this passage?** _____

   c. **In everyday language, what is God saying in this passage?** _____
   _____

   d. **Is God knowable according to this passage?** _____

If the God of the Universe could not be found; if He were not approachable; if He were not knowable; He would not tell His children to spend time seeking Him. Our attempts would be in vain.

THE VOICE OF TRUTH

6. **Read John 10:11.**

   a. **Who does Jesus say He is in this passage?** _____

   b. **Who are His sheep?** _____

7. **Read John 10:2-4**

   a. **Who hears His voice?** _____

   b. **How does the Shepherd call His sheep? (v3b)** _____

   c. **What does the Shepherd do after He calls them by name? (v4a)** _____

   d. **How do the sheep respond? (v4b)** _____

WEEK 5 | DAY 1

Whenever the Bible refers to a sheep/shepherd relationship, it is describing the relationship God intends for Jesus (The Good Shepherd) and His sheep, (those who are God's children) to enjoy.

Now notice, it does not say that the special sheep can hear His voice. It says, "His sheep listen for His voice." This refers to *all* the sheep. The Bible even says that He knows our name. In a world of 7 billion, how easy it is to feel unnoticed, unheard and unimportant. But the Bible says, He *knows us;* He *loves us;* He *sees us.* He sees us when no one else does. He sees when we are all alone and lonely. He sees when that knot forms in the back of our throat before bursting into tears. He sees when our stomach sinks and we get that nauseated feeling when disturbing news comes our way. He sees when we're perplexed and need direction. He sees when we're frustrated and need the ability to think straight. He loves us and wants to comfort and us and encourage us. He desires to direct us and guide us. Can you imagine how insulting it must be to Him when we run to others for help?

I'd like to share how the Good Shepherd has spoken to me from the pages of His Word. I've recorded these thoughts in my Prayer Journal, under the *Listening* section. Before we get started on this exercise, realize I may make a request and not immediately receive an answer. In fact, it may be days, weeks, months and in some instances, years before I "hear" my answer. However there are occasions – many occasions, I hear my answer that very day. Do not become discouraged when you do not initially hear Him addressing your situation or issue. However, God is faithful and He will speak. (I go into greater detail as to how to hear Him speak on Day 4 of this week).

DATE – WRITE THE DATE SITUATION	WHAT GOD SAID	MY RESPONSE
A knot is found by the doctor in my breast. Biopsy needed – fear overwhelms me the day before the procedure.	**John 14:27, "My peace I give you. Do not let your heart be troubled and do not be afraid."**	Unexplainable peace instead of fear. I wrote the verse down on a slip of paper and put it in my pocket. Every time fear rose up – I pulled out my Scripture and spoke it out loud. My peace became immoveable.
Knowing God Ministries becomes an official 501(c)3 organization. Now what? Fear of the unknown.	**Genesis 6,** God gave Noah specific, detailed instructions for building the ark.	Knowing God gave Noah such specific instructions comforted me knowing He'll do the same for me as long as I'm coming to Him for the blueprints.
Alliance with Christian company They did not kept their end of the contract – I feel cheated and mistreated. I know the Lord connected me with them. However, I can't help but feel thrown under the bus by God.	**Genesis 28-31,** God sent Jacob to Laban knowing he would be cheated and mistreated. Yet He provided and protected Jacob – just as He said He would in Genesis 28:15. It was for Jacob's good.	Just as God was preparing Jacob for his calling to become Israel, He was preparing me for my calling. God broke Jacob of his old ways and trained him in that difficult place. He intended to do the same with me.
Betrayed by someone I thought was my friend.	**Luke 6:27-28, "Love your enemies. Do good to those who hate you. Pray for those who hurt you."**	Chose to forgive and pray for her. The more I pray for her, the more compassion I feel towards her.
Fear of flying on a day that I was to take a flight out of town.	**Psalm 68:34, "Proclaim the power of God, whose power is in the skies."**	Peace over flying. Kept saying verse over and over whenever I felt fearful.

CREATED FOR PURPOSE

Date – Write the date Situation	What God Said	My Response
Call to write this Bible study – have been collecting data for 2 years	Ezekiel 3:24, "Go shut yourself up in your house. There you will be bound with ropes so that you cannot go out among the people." I knew God was calling me to a season of staying in my office.	I shut out the rest of the world with the exception of my family and focused entirely on the study. This was harder than you may think!
Operating table prior to anesthesia. Very fearful of being put under. This Bible verse jumps in my head:	Joshua 1:9, "Have I not commanded you? Be strong and courageous. Do not be terrified; do not be discouraged, for the Lord your God will be with you wherever you go."	Total peace as the mask goes over my face.

Do you see how personal, specific and relevant God is when we take our issues, our troubles, our broken hearts, our fears and our concerns to Him? He will speak to us personally – by name! He'll speak in a language we can understand. Yes, the context you may be reading is Paul speaking to the Galatian church. But all of a sudden, you'll read a phrase or a sentence or a paragraph that might as well have your name attached to it. It will address your circumstance and your issue in a way that connects your heart to God unlike anything else has the ability to do.

This is when you know that the God of the Universe in all His glory and splendor and majesty is speaking personally to you. Oh, the things He'll tell us, if we will just go to Him and then listen to what He has to say!

8. **Share when the Good Shepherd has spoken to you personally. (From Scripture) If you can't answer, no condemnation; It's why you're in the study!**

   _____

9. **How does today's lesson impact your preconceived ideas?**

   _____

Make no mistake about it, those who belong to Him are given the ability to hear His voice. Will you carve out the time to listen?

JOURNAL RESPONSE

Take a few moments to meditate on our study today.

Were there particular Scripture(s) or statement(s) that spoke to you personally?

1.

2.

3.

WEEK 5 | DAY 2

TODAY'S TREASURE
...
"AS FOR WHAT WAS SOWN ON GOOD SOIL, THIS IS HE WHO HEARS THE WORD AND GRASPS AND COMPREHENDS IT; HE INDEED BEARS FRUIT AND YIELDS IN ONE CASE A HUNDRED TIMES AS MUCH AS WAS SOWN, IN ANOTHER SIXTY TIMES AS MUCH, AND IN ANOTHER THIRTY."
MATTHEW 13:23 AMP

THE SOIL OF OUR HEART

There is nothing more secure and protecting than the sound of Jesus' voice spoken into the depths of my heart. His voice is comforting. It is gentle. It is not condemning, but sometimes it is direct. It is encouraging. It is soft. At other times, it is stern. His voice takes away my fear and replaces it with peace.

If we did not know each other and I were to call you on the phone, you would not know my voice. You would initially have to say, *"Who is this?"* However, if we became good friends, you would get used to the sound of my voice. Most likely, you would not have to ask who this is when I called. You would instinctively know.

So it is with Jesus. The more time we spend in His Word, the more we will know His voice directing and guiding us. However, we must be careful because the soil of our hearts matters a great deal.

SOIL TYPES

Last week, I asked what your heart attitude is toward God's Word. Your answer is important because it affects your hearing. If we have the wrong heart soil, we will not be able to hear personally from God. The good news is that our heart condition can change. But it's important to identify the specific soil our hearts represent. We will see how this is the precursor to living extraordinary lives.

MATTHEW 13:18-23 and Mark 4:13-20

1. What does the *"seed"* represent? _____

2. **God's Word falls upon 4 different types of *"heart soils."* Write out the soil types and what they represent.** _____

CREATED FOR PURPOSE

Soil Type #1: _____

What happens to the seed? _____

The first soil type represented is the seed sown along the path. The path in that day and age was the roadway people traveled, so it was hardened. The seed there was unable to take root, so the birds of the air came and snatched it up. The birds of the air represent Satan, the evil one, who comes and snatches the Word immediately upon hearing it.

Soil Type #2: _____

What does the soil represent? _____

What happens to the seed? _____

Soil Type #3: _____

What does the soil represent? _____

What happens to the seed? _____

The seed is the message about the Kingdom of God; God's Word. It falls on soil that is either as hard as concrete (the path) or rocky or overgrown with thorns. On all paths but the first, the Word seems to be well-received. However, life happens: we worry about unpaid bills, job loss, or the diagnosis of a disease. We perhaps grieve an untimely death, or are misled by the deceitfulness of the things we studied on Brainwashed Boulevard, which can also impact the seed.

3. **Name some of the items we studied on Brainwashed Boulevard. (You may have to look back @ Week 2)**

   _____

Remember when we discussed these items? None of them were bad things in and of themselves. However, if our roots in Jesus and His Word are shallow, these things choke the seed that was planted in:

    Our quiet time or
        the Sunday morning message, or
            the message we heard in Bible study and had every intention of applying.

But we got home… we got busy working or checking email or Facebook, or running errands. We had lunch or continued fellowship with girlfriends that drew us away from Christ rather than to Christ. We continued in our old habits by pursuing the pleasures of life and forgetting what we had heard, thus walking away from the seed that was planted, and never allowing it to take root in our hearts so that it could grow to maturity.

Upon leaving Bible study or church, what do you think about? Do you pick up your IPhone to check all your missed calls, messages or texts and begin actively engaging those? Do you haphazardly turn on the radio in your car and unintentionally drawn out the voice of your Shepherd? Are you so preoccupied with hunger that food and the nearest restaurant are the only things you can think about?

WEEK 5 | DAY 2

I've shared that I used to be in a Monday night Bible study. I can distinctly remember getting into my car one night following a lecture and, as was my habit, turning on the radio. All of a sudden, I sensed a quickening in my heart. It was the voice of my Shepherd, asking me if I wanted Him to solidify in my heart and mind what I had just heard, if I wanted to know how He wanted me to apply the message I had just heard to my everyday life.

From that night on, the drive from church to home became a time for quiet reflection, a time for Jesus to do His work within my heart in response to the seed that had just been sown. Was I dealing with jealousy or bitterness? Was I prompted to apologize to someone? Was I prompted to do something specific? Could the Lord be asking me to pray for my husband? Was He asking me to change my actions and attitude towards him? Could I have possibly gotten too busy with all my activities and failed to truly _hear_ my child's heart? Had my patience run low when I had to repeat myself to my husband who needs a hearing aid, but refuses to get one?

You see girlfriend, the seed is scattered. The seed falls, but what is the condition of the soil of our hearts in response to God's Word? Is the seed falling on the hard path? Is it on the rocky or thorny soil? Or is it falling on good soil, ready to receive the Word and apply the direction of the Lord?

THE ORDINARY BECOMING EXTRAORDINARY

4. **What is the fourth soil type?** _____

   What does the soil represent? _____

   What happens to the seed? _____

5. **Do you see a correlation between John 15:5 and the fourth *"heart soil"*? What is it? See Today's Treasure.**

   _____

I hope your answer included the word "fruitful."

When you and I hear God's Word and cling to it, allowing it to change our hearts, our minds, our attitudes, our preconceived ideas, our prejudices and our behavior – this is when the Word takes root. And as a result, it produces a harvest in our lives.

6. **What are the 3 levels of harvest?** _____

I don't know about you, but I'm not satisfied with a thirty-fold harvest. I want to be one who produces a hundred-fold. Because this, dear sister, is when we begin to significantly impact our corner of the world. This is when we say goodbye to mundane, mediocre, pew-sitting living, and begin truly living the life of purpose we were destined to have.

Again, we see it's all about the heart.

JOURNAL RESPONSE

Take a few moments to meditate on our study today.

Were there particular Scripture(s) or statement(s) that spoke to you personally?

1.

2.

3.

WEEK 5 | DAY 3

TODAY'S TREASURE
...
"THEN HE TURNED TO THE DISCIPLES AND SAID PRIVATELY... FOR I TELL YOU THAT MANY PROPHETS AND KINGS WANTED TO SEE WHAT YOU SEE BUT DID NOT SEE IT, AND TO HEAR WHAT YOU HEAR BUT DID NOT HEAR IT."
LUKE 10:23-24

HEARING FROM GOD PERSONALLY

One of the truths that I love about the Magi, in reference to the birth of Christ, is that God spoke to them differently than He spoke to Mary and Joseph. Yet God spoke to them in a language that they understood.[2]

He does the same today. He will speak to you and me in a language we understand, yet what He says will always reflect what is said in His Word. The Holy Spirit is the primary source that enables us to hear from God.[3] We will see this in our study today.

Following Jesus' death, burial, resurrection, and ascension, the Holy Spirit was sent at Pentecost to dwell in those who would receive Christ as Savior. When we became children of God, the Holy Spirit came to live within us.[4]

1. **John 14:16-17. How is the Holy Spirit described?**

   _____

   _____

2. **Where does the Holy Spirit live? (17b)**

   _____

   _____

---

2   Matthew 2:1
3   1 Corinthians 2:12
4   Ephesians 1:13-14

CREATED FOR PURPOSE

3. **John 14:26. What does the Holy Spirit do?**

   a. _____

   b. _____

4. **According to John 16:13, what else does the Holy Spirit do?**

   a. (v13a) _____

   b. (v13b) _____

   c. (v13c) _____

   d. (v14) _____

   e. (v14c) _____

If we spend time with the Lord, allowing Him to speak into the deep recesses of our heart, He will share with us the mind of God on any issue we desire to know about. The Holy Spirit will remind us of what we've studied or learned from the Bible when we are in a precarious or indecisive situation. We can count on Him to guide us in the direction God desires us to go. The Holy Spirit will even tell us what is yet to come. (When He does, it will always stay true to Scripture.) Above all, He brings glory to Jesus.

5. **How do Proverbs 4:5-6 and John 16:13 correlate with each other?**

   _____

The Guide will direct our paths if we'll allow Him. He'll remind us of God's ways and direct us to every path in life. All we have to do is acknowledge Him and listen to the quiet of our heart for direction.

WHERE DO WE START?

First of all, we have to know with great certainty, if we **are not** spending consistent, quality time with God in His Word, we will not be sure of His voice. We will wonder:

>   Is this my voice?
>   Or the voice of the enemy?
>   Or the voice of Jesus?

Now please don't get legalistic with this and think that if you miss your quiet time one day, all is doomed or you've disqualified yourself from hearing the Holy Spirit guide you that day. That is NOT how God operates. However, if it's been days or weeks since we've spent time with the Lord, that *"voice"* quite possibly may be YOUR voice or the enemy's voice. Don't forget, even if something sounds good, it doesn't always mean it's best. Satan masquerades as an angel of light[5] seeking to derail you from God's best. If it's been a few days or weeks, just come back into the loving arms of your Daddy – Abba (Father) in your quiet time spot!

---

5   2 Corinthians 11:14

WEEK 5 | DAY 3

For the last two years, I have been reading a Daily Chronological Bible (NLT). I have loved it! Each day, I feel like God has a new treasure for me hidden within. Although much of this Bible is Old Testament, I try to read a New Testament passage daily as well. I may read only a few verses, or I may read chapters at a time. I then pick up the next day from where I left off. There have been times that I'm days behind. But again, it's a relationship, not a religion. It's about quality, not quantity.

Now, what's working for me in my quiet time may not be where God wants you to spend your time. So here's the question you must ask yourself: Is the material I'm reading or studying *"sparking?"* Meaning, is what I'm reading capturing my heart and drawing me closer to Jesus? When a passage is sparking, it should leap off the page and into our hearts addressing our everyday *"stuff."* If not, it's time to change it up! Pray and ask the Lord what He wants you to study. And be listening for the Holy Spirit to guide you into the Truth He desires you to be in.

I love reading a Gospel (Matthew, Mark, Luke, and John) at all times. You may want to start with a different book in the Bible. Ask the Holy Spirit to show you.

Perhaps you are dealing with bitterness. If so, get a concordance and study all the verses that deal with forgiveness.[6] Perhaps you deal with feeling unloved and insecure. Study verses that deal with love.

Go to LifeWay or Family Christian or to your nearest Christian bookstore and find a book that deals with your issue. I would encourage you to pray before choosing a book, if this is the route you are taking, allowing the Holy Spirit to guide you while in the store. When reading a book in your quiet time, make sure it is Biblically based with Scripture throughout. During your quiet time, take notes and look up the passages of Scripture. You may even want to read around the Scriptures if doing that is *"sparking"* for you.

As much as I love certain devotionals and books and Bible studies, **nothing takes the place of the Word of God.** Please don't ever allow the enemy to fool you.

TEN MINUTES?

Perhaps your quiet time is a Daily Devotional. Many new believers start here. Daily Devotionals are great for both new and seasoned believers. However, I want to caution you. If all you give your quiet time is 10 quick minutes each day, the seed planted in your heart will only yield a very little amount. Ten quick minutes EVERY DAY is not enough for the Word to get in you, to become a part of you in a way that God desires. Ten quick minutes will most likely not be enough to lead you to the path and the life the Lord desires you to be on, much less give you the strength to stay and persevere once you get there.

This may sound harsh to some of you. But I only want to be honest. I don't want you to feel misled. Not to mention, how insulting this must be to the Lord when we only allocate 10 minutes of our day to Him. I know if my husband had this mentality, it would be very hurtful to me.

The really cool thing about Jesus is this: the MORE you know Him, the MORE you want to get to know Him better. When you're reading is "sparking," you'll look up and see that it's been 45 minutes or an hour and you'll wish there were more time.

I have a few devotionals that I really like. However, I use them as "spiritual vitamins," not as my main meal. I place them throughout the house and the car for easy reading when I get a moment, in such places as the end table in my den, my bedside table, the bathroom, and the center console of my car.

---

6 You can find wonderful concordances online now.

CREATED FOR PURPOSE

WONDERFUL TECHNOLOGY

Technology is a great thing. People today can look up Scriptures on their tablets, computers, and phones. We can open any translation of Scripture we choose to read. This is very handy and convenient.

Two things to remember: First, NOTHING replaces the actual Word of God sitting on your lap, with a piece of paper, pen, or Journal in tow so you ready to take notes. NOTHING can take its place. Be careful with technology – it can be very distracting.

Second, you must exercise great self-control not to check your email or texts when using these technologies. Whenever I check my email or texts prior to my quiet time, I've just opened Pandora's Box to the world. My ears are now in tune with the world. And now my mind may begin to gnaw on a frustrating or troubling email, or I may start trying to figure out how to answer a certain email. As hard as I try, I personally have a very difficult time transitioning to being wholeheartedly, fully in tune with what the Lord may be trying to say. My mind is now distracted.

Again, I don't mean to make a legalistic rule out of this; it's just something for you to consider.

6. Read Luke 10:23-24. Meditate on what this passage says. Write down what you glean from it...

_____

_____

I have a gal on my team who has been with me since its inception. Her name is Ellen. During our team meetings, we spend a great deal of time on our knees in prayer. She can find and pray some of the most profound Scriptures. One day, she prayed this passage (Luke 10:23-24) and it sparked like never before in my heart. The minute we got off our knees, I said, *"Ellen, where is that passage? That is mind-boggling!"*

Girlfriend, when you and I get serious about our relationship with the Lord, He will tell us things (privately – in our prayer time or quiet time) that kings and presidents long to hear. He'll give us wisdom, discernment, and insight that the President of the United States could only wish to have.[7]

7. Why do you think kings and presidents are not *"hearing"* as Jesus describes in verses 23-24?

_____

This is not to say that He will not speak to the leaders of the world, because HE will – if they ask; if they come to Him; if they'll believe; if they'll think they are not wise in their own eyes. He'll do this for all of us. But we must come to Him.

---

[7] If the president, or any other leader for that matter, seeks the Lord wholeheartedly, then he or she hears Jesus. But God does not share wisdom that could easily be ours unless we ask for that wisdom.

WEEK 5 | DAY 3

JOURNAL RESPONSE

Take a few moments to meditate on our study today.

Were there particular Scripture(s) or statement(s) that spoke to you personally?

1.

2.

3.

WEEK 5 | DAY 4

TODAY'S TREASURE
...
"HE WHO DWELLS IN THE SHELTER OF THE MOST HIGH WILL REST IN THE SHADOW OF THE ALMIGHTY."
PSALM 91:1

How to Hear His Voice

I am a very simple, ordinary person. Many of the women who have had profound impact on my spiritual growth rely heavily on the three point study method[8] in their quiet time. This is a very beneficial way to go deeper into God's Word, making it more and more applicable to everyday life.

However, I don't use this method very often. Sometimes I feel guilty because I'm not doing what *"they"* are doing. Surely if there were a formula or recipe for having a vibrant quiet time, and if I did the same thing they are doing, then I should get the same results, right? Not necessarily.

In this season of my life, that method makes me a little bored. But here's the thing the Lord has placed on my heart: I'm not to follow what *"they"* are doing; I'm merely to follow the Holy Spirit's leading. He will lead me into all Truth. So the lesson is, be careful of comparisons. Allow the Holy Spirit to direct your time with Him.

I have personally found that when I ***prayerfully*** begin my quiet time and then thoughtfully read the Word, I *"hear"* God speaking personally to me right from the pages of Scripture.

TIPS FOR HEARING GOD SPEAK

1. **Always open in prayer.**

2. **Expect to hear from the Lord each day.**

3. **Come to your quiet time with your circumstances in mind.**

4. **He'll speak, where you are. If you are reading a devotional, a book in the Bible, or a blog entry that is a devotional – expect Him to speak in that place.**

5. **If you go days without hearing Him speak, consider changing what you are reading. Ask the Lord to show you what He wants to teach you.**

---

[8] Discussed at length in my study, *Intimacy with God*; p173.

CIRCUMSTANCES IN MIND

Read Hebrews 11:6

1. What does it take to please God? _____

2. When we come to Him in our quiet time, we must believe _____ .

3. What does He do? _____ .

When your world is falling apart at the seams and you don't know which end is up or down – there is NO GREATER REWARD than to HEAR the God of the Universe who has the ability to change or alter your situation speak personally and practically into that situation. NOTHING is greater!

So come into your quiet time, believing that God will speak into your circumstances, questions or issues. Make sure you have those thoughts in mind. (Often I'll write my issues out in the bottom left side of my Prayer Journal, *Intimacy with God, Your Daily Guide to Prayer*. Then when I sense God has spoken to a particular issue, I'll write down His answer on the right side.)

Read with purpose (intentionally), and when suddenly something jumps off the page addressing the issues or fears or dilemmas that you may be facing that day or that season, don't chalk that arresting moment up to coincidence. Remember, you opened in prayer. You've asked God to speak… You've asked to share His thoughts and His concerns; to lead, direct and guide.

DWELL AND REST

Read Psalm 91:1-2

4. What do you think verse 1 means? _____
_____

5. How can I apply verse 2 means to my everyday life? _____
_____

Recently I attended my niece's basketball game. My sister, Heather, is her coach. After a recent game, several mothers complained about the playing time for their children. Heather is not a confrontational person. She struggles in this area. So when approached by some parents about the lack of minutes on the court for particular players, my sister felt judged, and felt she had upset the parents of the kids she has grown to love. She left the gym with her stomach in a knot.

The next morning, she woke up wondering what the best way to deal with unhappy parents might be. Because Heather is a Jesus girl, it has become her habit to *dwell* in her quiet time spot. That place in her home is the ***shelter of the Most High***.[9] She's not in a hurry. She doesn't rush through her quiet time as if she's punching a clock at work.

And because she has made God her ***Fortress and her Refuge*** – not her husband, as dear as he is, nor her children, nor her sister (me, the Bible Teacher who was in town visiting her when this happened), she sat down, prayed, and began expectantly reading, picking up from where had she left off the day before.

---
[9] For more on your quiet time place, see *Intimacy with God*, p. 67

That particular week, she had been reading a church blog that posted devotions associated with the current sermon series. The title of the devotional essay for that day was "Being Honest."

One of the sentences from the devotion that jumped out at Heather was, *"Although **confrontation may be uncomfortable, it is a vital way we can serve one another.**"*

She read the accompanying scripture, Philippians 2:3, *"Do nothing out of selfish ambition or vain conceit, **but in humility**, consider others better than yourselves."*

She asked the Lord, "What can I do to be humble toward these parents whom I felt attacked by last night?"

Suddenly an idea dropped into her heart: Send a humble email explaining the facts, and then give the parents the freedom to do whatever they desired even if that meant taking their girls off the team and putting them on another team.

So she immediately sent an email to the parents, explaining the facts, being honest and humble– doing her best to go the extra mile and serve even the difficult parents. There are 11 girls on a basketball team where only five can play at a time. She said she could only guarantee a quarter and a half of playing time for each girl, even though she had been working with the girls all season and had grown to love all of them. She ended by suggesting that *if parents preferred to move their daughters to another team* where they would have more playing time, they should feel free to move them to a team with fewer players. When Heather sent that message, she immediately felt the knot in her stomach lift, and her joy returned.

Because Heather has learned to ***dwell in the shelter of the Most High***, He brought ***rest to her soul***. Had she have gone to her husband or me or to anyone else, we would never have been able to give her the wisdom and the direction that the God of the Universe was ready to give her.

Do you see how personal, practical and relevant God will be if we'll only come to Him and not go by our own feelings?

IT'S NOT ABOUT FEELINGS

One of the greatest favors you can do for a friend when they come to you with a dilemma is to ask her, *"What has the Lord said about this issue? Have you taken it to Him?"*

Sadly, in the Body of Christ, at least in my corner of the world, an affirmative answer is a rarity. Quite often when I ask this question, people look at me like I have 3 heads! Or worse, the answer I get starts with the phrase, *"I feel like God is saying...Plus my circumstances are saying this too. This must be God."*

No, no. Not necessarily. Just because our circumstances are saying one thing does not mean that God is speaking through those circumstances. God can and does speak through circumstances, but He primarily speaks through His Word, allowing our circumstances to follow what His Word has said.[10]

So when I ask a friend what the Lord has said, I'm not looking for an answer that starts with, *"I feel."*[11] I'm looking for WHAT SPECIFICALLY HAS GOD SAID from His Word? He will speak. Have you carved out the time to listen? Are you listening?

Sweet sister – dear sweet sister -- we cannot live by our feelings, and we can't live by "following our heart," as the world so often tells us to do.

6. Read Jeremiah 17:9. How does it affirm the wisdom of not following your heart?

_____

---

10 See *Intimacy with God*, Runway Lights p. 171
11 This is discipling women in your corner of the world to take their "stuff" to Jesus.

"Follow your heart," says the world. *"Whatever feels good. Whatever will make you happy; this is what you should do. After all, life is about being happy."*

If this is our motto, we will never live the life God has destined for us. When we live by our feelings:

> we have affairs;
>> we leave our husbands;
>>> we wind up pregnant outside of marriage;
>>>> we live with our boyfriend who has no intention of marrying us;
>>> we become drug addicts (prescription or otherwise);
>> we become critical and judgmental towards others;
>>> we live in deep debt;
>>>> we become lazy;
>>>>> we become obese;
>>>> we begin looking at or reading about porn to get us in the mood.

God did not make us for happiness, but for holiness. DO NOT LIVE BY YOUR FEELINGS or mistake God's voice as what your feelings are dictating. It is not the way to a purpose-filled life of abundance in God.

We are promised that when we follow Jesus rather than our hearts; when we follow the Holy Spirit guiding and directing us:

> Our joy will be complete;
>> We will live in abundance;
>>> We will live a life far different than many other people…

Because when we begin saying, "No" to our flesh and "Yes" to Jesus, then we start living![12]

Yes, it may be uncomfortable for a period of time, but remember what God has promised to those who love Him:

> *"No eye has seen,*
> *no ear has heard,*
> *no mind has conceived*
> *what God has prepared for those who love Him." 1 Cor. 2:9*

---

[12] Galatians 5:24-25

WEEK 5 | DAY 4

JOURNAL RESPONSE

Take a few moments to meditate on our study today.

Were there particular Scripture(s) or statement(s) that spoke to you personally?

1.

2.

3.

REVIEW

1. What were the most meaningful or significant lessons you learned each day?

   Day 1: _____

   _____

   Day 2: _____

   _____

   Day 3: _____

   _____

   Day 4: _____

   _____

2. Is there anything you sense God telling you to do as a result of the study this week? If so, share.

   _____

   _____

3. What action steps do you need to take in order to be obedient?

   _____

   _____

6

OBEDIENCE IS KEY

WEEK SIX

Day 1 | Our Lineage

Day 2 | Lifestyle Change

Day 3 | The Power of Living Obediently

Day 4 | Baby Steps

Day 5 | Review

WEEK 6 | DAY 1

TODAY'S TREASURE
...
"NEITHER BEFORE NOR AFTER JOSIAH WAS THERE A KING LIKE HIM WHO TURNED TO THE LORD AS HE DID – WITH ALL HIS HEART AND WITH ALL HIS SOUL AND WITH ALL HIS STRENGTH."
2 KINGS 23:25

OUR LINEAGE

Throughout Scripture, God calls ordinary, average people to live extraordinary lives. Seth, Noah, Abraham, Rahab, Joseph, Moses, Joshua, Deborah, Samuel, Ruth, David, Huldah, Mary the mother of Jesus, Peter, Paul, Lydia, Priscilla, Mary Magdalene, Dorcas, Lois, and Eunice were flesh-and-blood people just like us. What made them extraordinary was the fact they listened to and followed the Lord's leading most every day of their lives. They obeyed in the little things as well as the big ones. As a result, their lives significantly impacted their corners of the world and future generations.

The God who called these people to live extraordinary lives back then does the same thing today. And as we've studied since Week 1, the necessary ingredient to bearing much fruit during our sojourn on Earth is an abiding relationship with Jesus. That relationship is crucial to living purposeful lives of significance before the eyes of God.

Today's lesson will center on the impact of our family lineage as it relates to our life purpose and how sometimes our lineage or heritage can deter us from God's best. When we live in relationship with Christ, allowing His Word to be central in our lives, we often realize that what we've always thought about religion or about God isn't necessarily true. If this describes you, it will take courage to recognize any false teaching that you may have inadvertently allowed to affect your life.

For the next few days, we'll study the very ordinary King Josiah. If Josiah's past role models were an indication of how he would lead, it would have been fair to suppose that he would merely follow the family example, possibly disqualifying himself from having God work mightily through him. Yet this is not what happened. Josiah chose an entirely different path than that of his forefathers. Instead of living a life of failure in the eyes of God, he was a huge success.

1. **How does God forever record Josiah's tenure as King? Read 2 Kings 23:25, Today's Treasure.**

   _____

Notice the verb *turned* in 2 Kings 23:25. We'll see that Josiah *turned* the spiritual tide of not only his life, but of an entire nation back to the Lord. But what did he have to turn from?

CREATED FOR PURPOSE

THE BEGINNING

READ 2 KINGS 22:1-7

2. How old was Josiah when he became king? _____

3. How long did he reign? _____

King Josiah grew up in the middle of many generations who were wicked and idolatrous. These kings had led the entire nation of Israel astray by turning to idol worship. Their example led the people whom they ruled to live lives from God's standards. These kings had also allowed pagan altars to be set up in the Temple of God. So in the eighteenth year of Josiah's reign, when he was 26 years old, he set out to repair the Temple of the Lord.

READ 2 KINGS 22:8-20

4. What is found during the repair of the temple? (v8) _____

5. What does Shaphan, the secretary, do upon finding the *"book"*? (v10) _____

6. How does King Josiah respond to the contents from within the *"book of the Law"*? (v11-13)

   _____

7. What is the first thing Josiah commands? (v12-13)

   _____

8. Several people spoke to a prophetess named _____. (v14)

9. Summarize what the prophetess said concerning the nation of Judah (v16-17)

   _____

10. Summarize what the prophetess says about the King of Judah (v19-20)

    _____

11. Why is King Josiah shown favor by the Lord? (v19)

    _____

When Josiah heard the Word of the Lord written in the book of the Law, he tore his clothing and wept because neither his life nor the lives of his people were in accord with God's holy standards. His heart was moved by God's Word, and Josiah responded in total humility. The extreme changes he would implement would take great courage and would make him far different from his predecessors. Keep in mind that these previous kings were not random people, but Josiah's own father and grandfather.

2 Kings 21:19-22

12. Looking back, how is his father remembered? (v20)

    _____

WEEK 6 | DAY 1

13. What was his father's heart toward God? (v20-22)

14. How is Josiah's grandfather remembered? (2 Kings 21:1,2)

15. List some of the evil practices for which Manasseh is remembered. (2 Kings 21:6-7, 11, 16)

16. From Today's Treasure and our reading thus far, what did Josiah turn from?

When you familiarize yourself with his family history, it seems nothing short of a miracle that Josiah is recorded as *"doing what was right in the eyes of the Lord."* Perhaps it was his mother's influence that gave him a fear of the Lord. Scripture does not tell us, but merely gives a brief description of his maternal lineage. We simply do not know.

But this we know, the soil of his heart was tender towards the Lord because he tore his clothes at the awareness of the sin of Judah. (2 Kings 22: 11) We also know human nature typically models what's lived in front of us – be it good or bad.

17. **Name different lifestyles or ways of thinking that we typically model as adults from what we have seen childhood.**

I'm only scratching the surface when I say that we typically model and accept as normal what we've seen adults whom we love and respect live out in front of us. What we've seen modeled often forms the standards with which we approach life. From the way we parent our children, to the way we respond to stress, to the way we spend money, to whether we accept other races and cultures, to the level of education we pursue, to the way we treat our husbands: all these things are examples of lifestyles we carry into adulthood.

The same is true in our approach to religion and the things of God. Think about your family heritage, and please do so gently. This exercise is not meant to bring strife into your family or condemnation upon your loved ones. But we'll never move forward with the Lord and our life purpose unless we are brave enough to understand whether what we've been taught our whole lives is based on the Word of God.

So as you think about your lineage and what you've learned in this study and others, as well as church… What was modeled to you as a child?

CREATED FOR PURPOSE

18. What is your spiritual lineage? What has been passed down to you concerning God's Word, church, and the things of God? Do you have a rich heritage of generations calling upon God's name? Do you have a heritage of *"Sunday morning"* Christianity? Do you have no church or religion at all?

- If we've seen a mother and a father who love the Lord with all their heart, mind, and soul, we are likely to model this for our own children, nieces, and nephews.

- If we've seen a mother and a father live one way for two hours on Sunday morning but then differently the rest of the week, we are likely to imitate the same behavior.

- If we've seen parents seek God only when things go sour in life, this is typically the example that we will also follow.

- If our parents have or had no regard for the Bible and the church, we are likely to feel the same way.

History tends to repeat itself. Our lineage typically reveals what we will become unless we decide to be that *"One Woman"* in our generation who acts differently. It requires great courage to recognize and reject worldly example without bringing judgment or condemnation on those who raised us. Often, they've only modeled what they saw growing up and have done the best they knew to do.

If you do not have a rich heritage of generations calling upon the name of the Lord, be encouraged – you could be the one to break the cycle, just as Josiah was. But the challenge is this: if our lineage is like Josiah's, we must have the courage to recognize it and the willingness to do something about that.

JOURNAL RESPONSE

Take a few moments to meditate on our study today.

Were there particular Scripture(s) or statement(s) that spoke to you personally?

1.

2.

3.

WEEK 6 | DAY 2

TODAY'S TREASURE

...

"FOR WE ARE GOD'S
FELLOW WORKERS."
1 CORINTHIANS 3:9

LIFESTYLE CHANGES

For many years I had a "pro choice" conviction with respect to the issue of abortion. It wasn't until I saw firsthand in God's Word that the God of the Universe says abortion is wrong (See Psalm 139:13-16)[1] that I changed my mind. Now, no matter how articulate the argument in favor of a woman's choice may be, I go back to what God has to say on the subject. Not only has God's Word impacted my conviction on this subject, but it also has impacted the way I vote in political contests. I simply cannot reconcile separating my personal life from God's Word at the ballot box. When we try to separate God from the rest of our lives, there is something amiss in our hearts.

After learning God's Word, Josiah knew that he and his people were not living according to God's standard. He learned the blessings they were missing and the disaster that was pending because they had intentionally walked away from God's standards by compromising their faith and worshipping the idols of the cultures around them. What is our response when we realize that our convictions and perhaps our lifestyles are far from God's standard?

RADICAL OBEDIENCE

READ 2 KINGS 23:1-25

1. **What did Josiah do in response to God's Word as it related the people? (v 1-3)**

   _____

Notice how Josiah was not timid. He did not seem to care what his people or his family thought. He was more concerned with what God thought. May the same be true of us as well!

2. **Summarize the actions Josiah embarked upon in response to hearing the standards set in God's Word (v4-25)**

   _____

   _____

   _____

I'm blown away by Josiah's radical obedience! The lengths to which Josiah went in order to turn a wayward lifestyle into a lifestyle that pleased God were nothing short of marvelous. Josiah was not lazy. Nor did

---

[1] This is one of many passages God used to show me His standard.

he waiver or compromise God's standard. He did not make excuses. He did not cling to any emotional attachments he may have had to some of the idols. In big things and little things, neither his resolve nor his efforts wavered. Josiah was resolute and determined to make things right in his sphere of influence.

3. What impresses you about Josiah's radical obedience to God's Word?

   _____

4. Are you willing to be as radical when the Bible exposes wrong choices you may be making?

   _____

Why do we hesitate or waver or compromise God's standard when by simply living according to that standard we could potentially turn our lives around? Pause for a minute and think about it.

> When things are going wrong in our lives…
> When our circumstances are more than we can bear…
> When there's no joy in our heart…
> When there's no peace in our mind…

I believe it's in moments like these that God is issuing us an invitation to look to Him and His standards to make things right, to possibly go as far as Josiah did and make an entire lifestyle change if that's what is necessary.

GOD'S GREATER PURPOSE

When my children were small, I often craved ALONE time, so my husband would give me a Saturday afternoon to myself. My standard practice was to go to one of my favorite lunch spots. I would read a good book, do my Bible study without distraction, and then go to a movie.

Sounds pretty harmless, doesn't it?

I had a personal conviction regarding R-rated movies, so the movies I chose were always rated either PG or PG-13, and preferably *"chick flicks."*

However, something would happen in my heart during my afternoon at the movies. The men on the screen were usually Mr. Perfect, and the women on the screen were usually Mrs. Perfect. When movie people faced a crisis, their perfect lives were restored at the end. After seeing all that, I'd leave discontent with my life and my husband. I'd come home angry and grumpy to a man who had lovingly devoted his whole afternoon to taking care of his children so that his wife could come back feeling refreshed. What I treat I was upon returning home!

Little did I know that the seeds of discontent could be sown even by a two-hour movie. The Lord put on my heart that just because a movie was not rated R did not mean that it was His best for me. Applying that insight to my life required changing a familiar and enjoyable habit, and, to be honest, I did not want to change. But I made the change out of obedience to what I sensed the Lord putting on my heart.

Following this change and after finding a new hobby, I began returning home rested and restored, full of gratitude for my husband's sacrifice.[2] (By the way, my other hobby became writing! Much of my first Bible Study, *Intimacy with God*, was written during these hours away.) Do you see how I would have missed

---
2   Many times he had even gone to the grocery store with two small children, unloaded the groceries, and cooked a wonderful meal. Talk about Mr. Perfect!

out on God's greater purpose if I would have been UNWILLING to make the change? God is such an amazing God! His standards are NEVER there to make us feel restricted, but to give us freedom and to engage us in His divine purposes.

5. **When God exposes lifestyles or convictions or forms of entertainment or friends that are far from His best, how do you respond: in *obedience*, or by letting the insight go and making excuses for your unwillingness to change?**

_____

THE WARNING OF LAZINESS

It makes me tired to think of the effort and time it must have required for King Josiah to do all he did. Time is a very precious commodity in our lives. So often, it seems easier to take an issue and just *"shove it under the rug"* or *"let it go"* than to actually address challenges like turning away from an unhealthy relationship, from being a workaholic, or from entertaining friends who draw you away from rather than toward God. Other issues can include things like unwillingness to forgive your mother-in-law, or failure to discern what to share and not share with your friends (so that you are not sharing private marital issues with your girlfriend or sister). You might also struggle with not demeaning your husband for the fact that his body requires intimacy.

6. **If you tend to make excuses rather than confront what God may be putting on your heart, what keeps you from responding in complete obedience?**

_____

Is it a fear of what others may think? Fear of being different or ridiculed? Is it laziness? Do you have a fear of being politically incorrect in our very politically correct society? I've also heard the phrase, *"We've always done it that way."* But this is just another excuse to not make the hard choices so we *shove [conflict] back under the rug*. Why do we make excuses when God is placing in our minds and hearts how to make our circumstances and our lives better merely by aligning our lifestyles with His standards?

God, who is all-knowing, knows that the seemingly harmless choices we often make are indeed toxic. And He knows where toxic choices lead us and our families. So in His goodness, He raises "red flags" in our lives to get our attention. Red flags look like:

- Discontentment and worry about our circumstances
- Fear that sets in when circumstances go from bad to worse
- Lack of joy in our hearts, which manifests itself as anger, frustration, nagging, and complaining.
- When His Word says one thing, but our lives contradict that – this is rebellion.
- If we are continually trying to control and manipulate something or somebody
- Insomnia – lack of sleep.

All of these things are red flags that God could be using to get our attention to turn the tide of our lives in another direction.

CREATED FOR PURPOSE

7. Currently, do you have any red flags in your life? _____

_____

8. What is God leading your heart to do? _____

_____

I can say from experience that obedience is sometimes extraordinarily hard. But when God puts something on your mind, He also gives you the grace and power to do it. So don't procrastinate, sweet friend. When we procrastinate, it only delays the flow of blessings that could be ours.

JOURNAL RESPONSE

Take a few moments to meditate on our study today.

Were there particular Scripture(s) or statement(s) that spoke to you personally?

1.

2.

3.

WEEK 6 | DAY 2

TODAY'S TREASURE
...
"BUT EVEN MORE BLESSED ARE ALL
WHO HEAR THE WORD OF GOD
AND PUT IT INTO PRACTICE."
LUKE 11:28 NLT

THE POWER OF LIVING OBEDIENTLY

Nothing will motivate you to obedience more than circumstances that are so bad, that if God doesn't intervene, hopelessness is sure to come. When trying times come our way, we are smart if we seek the Lord for the instruction and wisdom that can only come from God Himself. The good news is that He promises to instruct us and to help us. But our response to what He is placing on our hearts to do will often determine the degree of His intervention.

Read Psalm 32:8-9

1. **What are the 4 promises God makes in this passage? (v8)**

   _____

   _____

2. **What does God say to NOT do? (v9)**

   _____

3. **What does this mean in our everyday language?**

   _____

Don't be like a stubborn two-year-old child that insists on having her way. Often we do this when we seek the Lord and He gives us an answer that we'd prefer to NOT hear. For many years, I was that senseless mule that would not submit to the things God was placing on my heart, until I needed a break-through in my painful and overwhelming circumstances. The situation that confronted my family and me drove me to voluntarily place the bit and bridle in my mouth because I desperately needed God to do SOMETHING only He could do, and fast!

UNLOCKING THE DOOR FOR BREAK-THROUGH

I set out to seek God's will and to seek His guidance by spending more time in my quiet place than usual. As I was trying to discern my next move, a word kept coming to mind. It was a word I really didn't want to hear, yet I heard nothing but this word day after day in the recesses of my heart.

CREATED FOR PURPOSE

The word was *"Apologize."*

I knew what God was referring to. For 11 years, I had been like a child with her hands over her ears, refusing to listen, because 11 years prior, I had gossiped about a high school classmate to a mutual acquaintance who turned around and shared my slanderous words with that classmate. Within days of the conversation, I received a call from my high school classmate, who confronted me with the unkind things I had shared. (Talk about being busted!) Did I 'fess up? Sadly, no. I lied and denied everything, saying, *"We're friends… Why would I do such a thing?"*

Funny, the things we'll do to cover our tails when we're put on the spot.

For the 11 years following that fateful conversation, I was slowly growing in my relationship with the Lord. From time to time, He would impress on my heart that I should reach out and apologize to this woman. But I would rationalize away the need for that apology by thinking to myself that *"The Lord would never tell me to do this. He would never want to embarrass me like this."* Not to mention, I thought, this is water under the bridge. Time to move on. It's in the past – forget about it!"

But one July morning in 2006, I could not escape the pressing that I sensed from the Holy Spirit telling me to apologize. If obeying what I sensed the Lord was saying would bring a breakthrough to my circumstances, I was willing to do anything. I desperately needed the Lord's guidance, and I DESPERATELY needed a breakthrough in the horrendous circumstances we were plagued with.

So at 9:00 a.m., following my quiet time that day, I looked up her phone number and called her. There was no answer. I hung up. I heard in my heart, *"Leave a message."* Uggh, I thought, I don't want to do that. I called back scared that she would answer this time. Still no answer. Relieved, I left a message.

After several days without a response from her, I thought I was off the hook, but I sensed the Lord telling me to write her a note. *"Haven't I done enough?"* I asked the Lord. *"After all, I have not seen this girl in 11 years – I've called – if she won't call me back, that's her problem, not mine."* *"Write a note of repentance and apology,"* The interior message came while I was walking my dog on a Friday evening.

As soon as I got home, I didn't even get a glass of water. I wrote the note. I confessed everything that I had said and lied about, telling her that I had a relationship with God now and that He had impressed upon my heart to apologize after all these years. I asked for her forgiveness, signed my name, and put it in the mailbox.

Suddenly, it was as if bricks came off of my shoulders. Oh girl, there was a refreshing of my spirit that I cannot describe. It was almost tangible. Inner joy and peace that sprung into existence right there at the end of my driveway. I may have skipped back to the door – I don't know! It just felt so good!

Within a month, breakthrough came.

OBEDIENCE IS POWERFUL

4. How does Jesus describe the person in Luke 11:28? _____

5. What qualifies a person for bringing greater blessing into his or her lives?

_____

Don't miss it, the person whom Jesus describes as even more blessed is spending time to hear the Word of God and then put that Word into practice.

WEEK 6 | DAY 3

6. Read John 14:21,23. How does Jesus quantify sincere love for Him?

_____

7. Read James 1:22-25. What does James urge us to do? (v22)

_____

THE FLAVOR OF THE WEEK

Oh, how easy it is to go to church or to go to Bible study and learn these awesome lessons. Then go about life as usual, never connecting the Word to our everyday life circumstances. In other words, just going about business as usual. Then we go back to Bible study – learn another awesome lesson and repeat the same habit.

I did this for years. I treated awesome, potentially life-changing lessons as though they were flavors of the week at Baskin-Robbins. One ice cream flavor might be the armor of God; another might be prayer; the week after that might feature knowing the will of God or understanding forgiveness. Each flavor was awesome, but I took none of them to heart. Even when the Baskin-Robbins metaphor did not quite fit, I treated incredible lessons like notches on my belt or took them for granted because they were nothing more than educational lesson .

8. How does James describe this mentality? (1:23-24) _____

The same thing is true with our quiet time. We can have a powerful quiet time, but then rise and walk away, forgetting what we just read.

9. The person who is _"blessed in what he does,"_ requires what 3 things? (James 1:25 NIV)

    a. "…looks _____ into the perfect law that gives _____.

    b. _____ to do this… _____ _____ what he has heard,

    c. but _____ _____."

Did you notice the word _freedom_? Who doesn't need freedom in their hearts, minds and souls? Freedom in emotions, circumstances, or finances? God's Word is the source of freedom. When we live the Word on the anvil of everyday life, we'll begin to experience this refreshing, empowering freedom. Yet this isn't how the world describes God's Word. It's more often ignored or described as confining, restrictive, or limiting. Don't be sucked in to the world's way of thinking!

10. Name the things that God has put on your heart to do (Even the practical things. God can be very practical with us.)

_____

11. Do you need a bit and a bridle placed in your mouth before you will walk in obedience?

_____

CREATED FOR PURPOSE

12. What holds you back from walking in consistent, complete obedience?

_____

Oh, sweet friend, if we'll cultivate a lifestyle of listening to and obeying what we sense the Lord saying, freedom and blessings upon our lives are promised! Do you see the power of obedience? Obedience is key to living and maintaining a purpose-filled life.

JOURNAL RESPONSE

Take a few moments to meditate on our study today.

Were there particular Scripture(s) or statement(s) that spoke to you personally?

1.

2.

3.

WEEK 6 | DAY 3

TODAY'S TREASURE

...

"FOR WE ARE GOD'S
FELLOW WORKERS."
1 Corinthians 3:9

Baby Steps

Living a dynamic purpose-filled life starts with baby steps behind closed doors where no one but God can see. My first baby steps of living a life purpose started by learning how to behave in my home. At the time, doing that was out of my comfort zone. Sometimes it still is!

The Bible says that wives are to help, respect, submit to, and sleep with their husbands. We are also told not to nag. So when I first began understanding my job description as a wife, I was far from my comfort zone. I much preferred to win arguments by having the last word, and I would sometimes control my husband through manipulation. Most of my habits were based on how I felt, and were not healthy in helping to build a marriage that would endure. Changing my home habits was the genesis of my purpose-filled life. If I couldn't obey God in the small things, how could He trust me with larger things?

1. How does Luke 16:10 speak to our obedience with little things?

_____

OBEDIENCE IN THE SMALL THINGS

Before I could be trusted with larger things in the kingdom of God, my stewardship was tested in the smaller things. The smaller things happened to be God's core priorities for any married woman with young children:

    A. My relationship with God – was it thriving or mundane?

    B. My relationship with my husband – was I living God's standard within the walls of my home?

    C. Parenting my children to be Christ-followers rather than just pew sitters.

    D. Practicing good stewardship over my home and resources.

    E. Living with excellence rather than sloppy mediocrity where God has given me stewardship.

CREATED FOR PURPOSE

Some of today's feminists would be utterly repulsed by much of the above list. Sorry if this offends, but these are God's standards, not mine. And we clearly see from Scripture that living out God's purposes on a larger scale ALWAYS begins on a much smaller scale.

> So make a decision to obey God in:
> your entertainment,
> your finances,
> your mind,
> your mouth, hands, and feet,
> your time,
> your attitude,
> your relationships...

God will give you the supernatural grace and power to do what He's asking you to do. Because He says we must bless and not curse our enemies, He gives us the grace and power to bless and not curse our enemies. Because we are told to forgive those who hurt us, God gives us the grace and power to forgive. It's where God has already given us stewardship that a life of purpose begins.

STEWARDSHIP

What comes to your mind when you hear the word "stewardship"? Do you think of money or finances? I used to think of stewardship in exclusively financial terms. However, stewardship is much more than that. Stewardship starts by identifying who is the owner of all things.

2. Who is owner of all things? (Psalm 24:1-2)

_____

God owns everything. And by God's grace, He allows us to manage everything He's entrusted to our care, be it finances, children, possessions, jobs, areas of influence, abilities, or talents.

3. How does 1 Corinthians 3:9 shed light on the definition of stewardship?

_____

Stewardship defines our purpose in this world as assigned by God Himself. Just as the seasons change, our seasons in life change as well. My God-given purpose in one season may become something entirely different in another season. This is why I've spent so much time talking about our quiet time and the importance of not neglecting it. It is in our quiet time that God reveals whether the winds of a new season are blowing our way. At that point, it is our divinely-given opportunity to join God in the work He reveals, or if He's ending a season of service – to step out.[3] Stewardship is our practical obedience in the administration of everything He's placed under our control for any given season.

4. Who and what has God entrusted to you in this season? Be as specific as possible.

_____

_____

---

3   This was a concept I learned in Henry Blackaby and Claude King's, *Experiencing God*.

WEEK 6 | DAY 4

5. **Do you have a clear conscience before the Lord that you are being a good steward of all of things or people in your charge? If not, what can you change?**

   _____

If you are married, He's entrusted a man and a covenant to you. If you have children, God has entrusted their spiritual development and upbringing to you. Are you a grandmother? An aunt? As far as it goes with you, are you doing your best to invest in having a meaningful relationship with your grandchildren or nieces or nephews for the purpose of drawing them to know God more personally?

Are you an employer, manager, or supervisor? Do you treat your people with respect and operate with integrity? Do you live the Bible before them as best you know how? Are you Christ-like even in little things like praying before you eat, or not taking part in the office gossip and drama?

Are you an employee? Do you work for your employer as though you were working for God Himself? Or do you steal your employer's time by roaming the Internet with your cell phone or texting your friends? Do you arrive at work on time? Do you take long lunches and leave early?

Do people look up to you as a role model in church or in your community? Are you doing your best to live above reproach?

Are you a youth counselor? Bible study leader? Sunday School teacher? sports coach? Do you take time to pray for the people whom God has entrusted to you during this season? Gently I ask, do you even care about what is going on in other people's lives? An indicator of whether you do is when you leave a conversation, do you look back afterward and realize that you talked the whole time? (I know these are thought-provoking questions. I ask because I deal with these issues.)

Are you willing to pour yourself into other lives by mentoring people or merely making yourself available to them, or are you too busy because you have too much on your plate? Do you prayerfully prepare for your lesson throughout the week or at the last minute if at all? Do you show up on time or are you consistently late to your commitments? What about with your finances and resources? Are you stingy? Or do you give freely? Are you so in debt that you feel restricted from giving?

What about the gifts, talents and abilities you've been given? How are you using them to serve God in the opportunities that come your way? What about your integrity? Do you consistently do the right thing even when no one else is watching?

6. **On a scale from 1-10 (10 being best), rate your stewardship in the following areas:**

Being a wife	1	2	3	4	5	6	7	8	9	10
Being a mom	1	2	3	4	5	6	7	8	9	10
Being an aunt	1	2	3	4	5	6	7	8	9	10
Being a grandmother	1	2	3	4	5	6	7	8	9	10
Being an employee	1	2	3	4	5	6	7	8	9	10
Being an employer	1	2	3	4	5	6	7	8	9	10
eing a community leader	1	2	3	4	5	6	7	8	9	10
Being a church leader	1	2	3	4	5	6	7	8	9	10
Handling your finances Handling your finances	1	2	3	4	5	6	7	8	9	10
Using your talents and abilities	1	2	3	4	5	6	7	8	9	10

CREATED FOR PURPOSE

SAYING NO

We women typically have a *"no"* problem. We hate to say no. (If you do not have this problem, consider yourself blessed. This is a major issue for many of us.) We overcommit ourselves by saying *"yes"* to everything from school activities to church activities to sports activities to activities with our girlfriends. Before long, we have so much on our plate, that we aren't doing anything well, let alone to the excellence of the Lord. And the people we love most pay the price, with our activities receiving most of our attention; our children usually fall in line next and our husband is last.

Our seasons of life will determine our availability:

- A young single woman, a middle-aged single woman, and a widowed woman represent three different seasons in life.

- A woman with a husband and grown children out of the house

- A woman with a husband and children still in the home

- A woman with a husband and small children

Each woman in the list above has a different kind of availability because each is in a different season of life with a different purpose.

7. Why does God desire to prune? John 15:2-3

_____

We must learn to say NO! As we spend time with the Lord each day, He'll reveal the activities that need to be pruned. At that point, we must obey what we sense Him saying and remove ourselves from the people or activities He is pruning. It does not always happen this way, but in my experience when God is pruning a certain activity or area of service, He'll take the joy we used to have with that away. Often, something that was easy will now be really hard and I'll begin to dread having to do it. Yet, once I remove myself, there's a feeling of relief. When we really think about it, why would we want to continue in activities that are bearing no fruit in our lives?

8. What is the initial command God gives to Adam and Eve? Genesis 1:28a

_____

Notice He does not say, *"Be busy and run around like a chicken with your head cut off!"* He says, *"Be fruitful and multiply."* And yes, multiplication can mean having natural born (biological) children, but it can also mean having spiritual children. A spiritual child is a person whom we mentor and lead to greater depth of relationship in Christ.[4]

9. What is one of the things that Jesus says we are to multiply? Matthew 28:19-20

_____

Jesus calls us to multiply disciples in our corner of the world – not just make converts. Let me explain what I mean: People become believers in Christ and often have no one to personally help them grow up in their new faith. A thorn rises up and chokes the seed that was sown and they fall by the wayside as revealed

---
4   1 Corinthians 4:15-16

in our study of the soil. Unfortunately, we all know people that have become believers, but are no longer serving the Lord, and often we cannot tell the difference between them and an unbeliever.

My heart aches for the woman who accepts Christ and has no one to teach her how to be a wife, a mom, and a daughter of God.

Oh, the difference we could make in our corners of the world if we adopted and lived by God's freedom-giving standards! The people in our sphere of influence who do not know Jesus will then want to know our Jesus, but not because we are Ms. Perfect or Ms. Holier-than-thou, and not because of our condemning nature. Friends and acquaintances want to know Jesus:

- Because of our selflessness towards others that speaks volumes in a selfish -what's-in-it-for-me kind of world.

- Because of our unwavering standards in a wishy-washy, poll-driven culture.

- Because of our joy even when things aren't going our way.

- Because of our supernatural peace and trust in God when a tsunami storms the beaches of our life.

- Because we're plugged into the Holy Spirit and know when to keep our mouth closed and when to speak.

- Because when we do open our mouth, we do not boast, but we gently share the ways that God is showing up in everyday circumstances and blessing us

- Because of our gentle, quiet spirit[5] that attracts people who would have been repulsed by "Sister Super Christian" and what they perceive as her self-righteous Bible-thumping.

This, dear friend, is when we begin living lives that matter – fruitful lives in our corners of the world. The virtuous influence partially catalogued above IS only possible when we are remaining on the Vine rather than beside it.

JOURNAL RESPONSE

Take a few moments to meditate on our study today.

Were there particular Scripture(s) or statement(s) that spoke to you personally?

1.

2.

3.

---

[5] 1 Peter 3:4

WEEK 6 | DAY 5

REVIEW

1. What were the most meaningful or significant lessons you learned each day?

   Day 1: _____

   _____

   Day 2: _____

   _____

   Day 3: _____

   _____

   Day 4: _____

   _____

2. Is there anything you sense God telling you to do as a result of the study this week? If so, share.

   _____

   _____

3. What action steps do you need to take in order to be obedient?

   _____

   _____

7

FINISHING THE
RACE

WEEK SEVEN

Day 1 | Your Talents and Abilities

Day 2 | Taking the *"Jesus Thing"* Too Far

Day 3 | Dream Again

Day 4 | Run so as to Win the Prize

Day 5 | Review

WEEK 7 | DAY 1

TODAY'S TREASURE

...

"PAY CLOSE ATTENTION TO WHAT YOU HEAR. THE CLOSER YOU LISTEN, THE MORE UNDERSTANDING YOU WILL BE GIVEN – AND YOU WILL RECEIVE EVEN MORE."
MARK 4:24 NLT

YOUR TALENTS AND ABILITIES

I was a leader serving in Christian leadership and had no idea how to pray. Prayer was overwhelming due to all the things that I needed to pray for. As I often do when overwhelmed, I did nothing, and just didn't pray at all.

So, one day, I confessed this to my dear friend and mentor, Maggie, who wisely advised me to divide my prayer needs by the days of the week, and then just pray a little each day. I loved the idea, so I went to the Christian bookstore in town and looked for a prayer journal that was organized by the days of the week. I could not find one. Ultimately, I ended up making my own out of an address book.

For two years, God taught me how to pray using this little homemade prayer journal. With each new facet He would teach me about prayer (praise, thanksgiving, confession, etc.), I would add a new section to my homemade journal.

MORE GIVEN

1. **What does Mark 4:24 (Today's Treasure) tell us will happen when we pay close attention to what Jesus is saying to us?**

   _____

When we obey what we sense God telling us to do, greater revelation will come.

In the weeks following my humiliating apology to the high school classmate whom I had slandered years before, I continued to spend a great deal of time with Jesus. My family was facing circumstances that were very painful and out of our control. I needed to hear from God Himself. I needed direction. I needed guidance. I needed to know what to do next in order to help my husband. Bottom line: I needed greater revelation.

In my quiet time one morning, suddenly, the same voice that had said, *"Apologize,"* now said, *"Publish your prayer journal."*

"Publish my prayer journal?" I said aloud. *"But that would be in direct conflict with what we actually need,"* I told God that morning. *"But because I don't want to ignore your voice, you'll need to tell my husband also, if this is indeed what You are telling me to do. I would have to have his approval if I'm hearing You correctly."* I did not think that my husband would agree due to our circumstances, but he was surprisingly supportive and encouraged me to publish my homemade prayer journal.

God seemed to give me word after word in my quiet time each day, confirming His path and purpose from Scripture. He said things such as, *"Get your supplies ready."* (Joshua 1:11). Meaning to me, *"find the vendors who could turn this into a reality."* (Publishing the original version of my prayer journal required three vendors: a binder vendor, a tab vendor, and a paper vendor).

God also said, *"She considers a field and buys it; out of her earnings she plants a vineyard."* (Proverbs 31:16) When God said this, I knew deep within my soul that the *"vineyard"* would be a women's ministry. I knew that out of the proceeds from the publishing of the prayer journal, I was to plant a vineyard and make it a fruitful place where women could come to know God personally.

Little did I know that the vineyard's name would become *Knowing God Ministries*. At this writing, the life-sustaining fruit that comes from that vineyard includes:

- A 501(c)3 tax exempt non-profit ministry.

- A devoted volunteer staff of 7 women who meet consistently for prayer about the direction and scope of the ministry, and a Board of Directors of 8.

- A website where vital resources for a woman's spiritual growth are available.

- A 3-year consistent devotional blog that suggests practical ways to know God personally in everyday life.

- A speaking ministry that started in 2007 that has crossed state lines and denominational barriers. By God's grace, we hope to add additional speakers.

- A statewide Women's luncheon called Iron Sharpens Iron, hosted regularly in the Raleigh/Cary, NC area for the last two years. At these luncheons, we teach women how to pray as we pray together. We also host a guest speaker who shares truth about the four main areas of a woman's life: her relationship with Jesus; her marriage; her parenting, and her ministry.

Still, "Publish my prayer journal?" I thought when God first dropped this in my heart. I had not written anything since my final term papers in college. I didn't know what to do or where to start.

So I delayed yet again because I felt overwhelmed.

Two months later, the words seemed to jump off the page of my Bible and into my heart when reading the account of Jesus feeding the 5,000 with five loaves of bread and two fish. Jesus seemed to be saying, "Tara, bring Me your little bits: Your *little bit* of knowledge, your *little bit* of creativity, your little bit of money for doing this project, and your little bit of time since you have children who are 4 and 2. I'll take your *little bit*, bless it, and feed a multitude.[1]

Nine months later, the prayer journal, *Intimacy with God: Your Daily Guide to Prayer*, was released. I was blown away by how many copies of that prayer journal that God sold, and the number of people whose prayer lives were changing. Two years later, the Bible study, *Intimacy with God: Establishing a Vibrant Quiet Time and Prayer Time* was self-published. Again, I marvel at how God has uses a fearful introvert

---

[1] John 6:10-13

WEEK 7 | DAY 1

to help women know how to have a personal quiet time, thus knowing God more intimately. This is one way that He's allowed me to multiply disciples in my corner of the world.

You see how my story started. Yours will blossom, too, when you are willing to bring Jesus every little bit of talent and ability.

YOUR TALENTS AND ABILITIES

Read Matthew 25:14-30

2. What does the man on the journey do? (v14) Fill in the blanks. "…who _____ his servants and _____ His _____ to them.

3. How does entrusting His property affirm the principle of stewardship?

   _____

4. Talents were given according to what determining factor? (v15) _____

5. Talents were given to 3 servants prior to the master's departure.

   a. How many talents was Servant 1 given? _____

   What did this servant do with what he was given? _____

   _____

   b. How many talents was Servant 2 given? _____

   What did this servant do with what he was given? _____

   c. How many talents was Servant 3 given? _____

   What did this servant do with what was given? _____

   _____

   Why? (v24-25) _____

I want you to see two distinct things from our study today.

CALLED

#1: Scripture says he *called his servants together and gave them different amounts of money to handle, according to their abilities*. Don't miss the fact that the master called the servants to himself. I picture him gathering his servants together to give them instructions about his plans and their purpose. What if one of the servants refused to go to the meeting, refused to hear what the master had to say?

When we continually refuse to meet with the Lord privately, we will never fully know our calling in life. Time with the Master is critical for receiving instruction as to how He wants us to use our talents and abilities.

ENTRUSTED

#2: The master in the parable also *entrusted his property* to his servants. Just as we studied stewardship at the end of last week, don't miss that He also entrusts us with gifts and His call that are irrevocable.[2] It's up to us to spend time with God, finding the gifts He's entrusted to us and where He wants us to use them. If we NEVER recognize our gifts and His callings, I believe it will be a sad day in heaven as we will quickly see that God had so much more planned for us – but we were either too lazy or too indifferent to realize the heart of the Father for our lives here on earth.

6. How long was the master gone? (v19) _____

7. How does the phrase settled accounts with them upon His return remind you of the believers judgment day from Week 2/Day 1?

    _____

Oh, girl, there will be a day when all accounts are settled! There is no doubt that the first and second servants did the best they could with what they were given. They used their stewardship for good, hence reaping the reward of gold, silver and costly stones. (1 Cor. 3:10-15)

8. How did the master respond to servants 1 and 2? (v21, 23)

    _____

9. What did the master call servant 3? (v26) _____

10. What did that servant do with his talents? _____

The third servant wasted his talents and abilities, in effect building his life on wood, hay, and straw… which if you remember, we can have a saved soul, yet a wasted life. (1 Cor. 3:10-15)

---

[2] Romans 11:29

Sadly, many people are like the third servant. They never connect with their Creator to find His purposes for them, or they hide their talents out of fear.

> Fear of responsibility;
> Fear of judgment;
> Fear of what other people may think;
> Fear of stepping out of their comfort zones;
> Fear of failure;
> Fear of rejection;
> Fear of hard work and sacrifice.

Let's face it; sometimes, we're just plain afraid that people will think we are taking this *Jesus thing* just a little too far.

JOURNAL RESPONSE

Take a few moments to meditate on our study today.

Were there particular Scripture(s) or statement(s) that spoke to you personally?

1.

2.

3.

WEEK 7 | DAY 2

TODAY'S TREASURE
...
"...LET US RUN THE RACE WITH PERSEVERANCE, THE RACE MARKED OUT FOR US."
HEBREWS 12:1

TAKING THE "JESUS THING" TOO FAR

When we begin allowing the Bible, rather than our feelings or public opinion, direct our decisions, big or small, we will stand out from the crowd in our corners of the world. After studying Josiah last week, I wonder: Did anyone accuse him of being narrow-minded or intolerant? DId his family members and close friends ever say in a very condescending tone, *"You're just taking this God thing a little too far."*

Since starting *Knowing God Ministries*, I've not heard that said to me personally, but I've certainly felt that implication. No harm is meant, yet the enemy has a way of twisting words to sting the heart in such a way that you end up questioning every act of obedience.

Today, I'd like to identify four specific obstacles that I personally have encountered. You may have encountered others. However, I believe when these obstacles are identified, we will have the strength to move on in courageous obedience.

OBSTACLES TO FOLLOWING HARD AFTER GOD

1. **Fear of what others think.**

    a. **Summarize Galatians 1:10:**

    _____

Are you afraid of what God might ask you to do? Afraid of where He might lead you if you were to start using your gifts and talents? Are you afraid of what He might ask you to give up? Afraid He'll embarrass you in front of your friends?

Everything I've just listed was a reason for my holding back from truly following the Holy Spirit, our guide. But remember from a few weeks ago, when I spoke of the path change and the verse that arrested my heart? Listen to it again. Apply it afresh to your own circumstances:

"I am the Lord your God, who teaches you what is best for you, who directs you in the way you should go. If only you had paid attention to my commands, your peace would have been like a river, your righteousness like the waves of the sea." Isaiah 48:17-18

Who are you more fearful of, God or Man? Are you concerned about acceptance in your neighborhood? Workplace? If we have an unbalanced approach and need other people's approval, this will ultimately steal our destinies and will make it impossible to truly live the purpose-filled life that God has planned for us. As hard as it is, especially if you were formerly Ms. Popular, you just need to go ahead and accept as fact that when you begin to follow Jesus wholeheartedly, you will be left out of certain circles, sadly even in some churches.[3]

    b.   **How could Psalm 118:6-8 encourage you and strengthen you?**

_____

We may not be able to see Him, but the Word says He is there – with us; ready to help; ready to intervene – so what can man do to me?

Yes, I'm left out of many of my former social circles. I quit *"Bunco,"* because I sensed the *no longer accepted feeling* from others when I wouldn't get tipsy-drunk on girls' night anymore. I left my children's playgroup when I refused to join in the ongoing *"what a bone-head my husband is"* conversation. The silence can be deafening when out to dinner with a group of women and you're the only one courageously speaking the truth about everyday issues. In lieu of speaking up, it would be far easier to remain silent and politically correct so that you can just fit in. However, please know that all I've lost socially is NOTHING compared to what I've gained in return. God is so faithful when we courageously WALK the TALK.[4] The same will be true for you as well!

2.   Fear of your past.

    a.   **How did Paul's past follow Him for many years in ministry? Galatians 1:23**

_____

Paul's reputation followed him like a Scarlet Letter. For many years, he had to convince those he was ministering to that he was not *"that person"* (persecuting and legalistic in the name of religion) anymore. Yet, Paul had confidence in *Who* had called him.

    b.   **Who had called Paul? Galatians 1:1** _____

    c.   **Who had not? (Gal.1:1)** _____

Be ready for other people to remember the *former you*. But remember, this is not you as you are now. Just as Paul received God's forgiveness and recognized that it was God who gave him his purpose, God does the same thing for us today. We too cannot allow our past to derail the future God has planned for us.

Even Jesus Himself was not accepted in his hometown.[5]

3.   Fear of the unknown.

    a.   **How does Galatians 5:25 command us to live?** _____

If we are living in step with the Spirit of God, we have nothing to fear. Therefore, be willing to follow wherever the Spirit might lead with wholehearted obedience.[6] Though we may not know what lies ahead,

---

3   The church girl will view the Jesus girl as radical, and taking the *"Jesus stuff just a bit too far."* Luke 6:22

4   Our lifestyles can say far more than our words if we'll stay close to Jesus, cultivating a gentle and quiet spirit which is of great worth in His sight (1 Peter 3:4). He'll also empower us to love those who do not necessarily love us. His Word says, *Love deeply, for it covers a multitude of sin.*(1 Peter 4:8)

5   Luke 4:24

6   Wholehearted obedience is holding nothing back – obeying to the very best you know how.

WEEK 7 | DAY 2

the Lord knows, and that's enough! We may miss out on some of His richest blessings if we insist on walking by sight, instead of by faith.

By keeping in step with the Spirit, you will be led down the very path marked for you.

    b. **How does Hebrews 12:1b indicate that there is a specific path chosen for each of us personally?**

_____

I love the phrase, *"the race marked for us."* That's my race, not my girlfriend's race, and not the race of someone whom I admire and want to emulate. God has a predetermined path for each of us, a path that He has planned for us to use our gifts and talents.

    c. **What is required for staying on that path? Hebrews 12:1-2**

_____

Throw off the fear of the unknown, or the fear of what others think, or anything else that hinders you from living the purpose-filled life of God. The secret is found by fixing our eyes on Jesus, the Author and Perfector of our faith. And one more thing:

    d. **Read 2 Corinthians 5:7. We walk by _____, not by _____.**

I often take comfort when I can't *"see."* Walking by faith and not by sight is something that gets God's attention almost more than anything else. He loves our willingness to be blindly obedient to Him and His Word alone. And I have found time and time again, that if I'm walking by faith on the wrong path, He GENTLY moves me to the correct path.

How does He gently move me? I'll read something in His Word that contradicts what I'm doing, or He'll send a more mature believer to confirm the correct path. And finally, I have a peace in my heart that cannot be described. (Listen to the peace in your heart. If you lack peace – put on the brakes!)[7]

FEAR OF LIVING OUT OF YOUR COMFORT ZONE.

The first few times I started speaking publicly, I would literally feel nauseated, as if I were going to be sick at any minute. The host would be introducing me from the platform, and I'd be mentally tuned out and trying to figure out where the bathroom was! Yet, from the moment I somehow summoned the courage to walk on stage, sharing the message God had given me to share, I instinctively began knowing that I'm doing what God called me to do.

If you and I continue to live safely in our comfort zones, we'll never know the thrill of seeing God work beyond our natural abilities. Following Jesus each day is not about our natural ability or strength; It's about staying close to Him so that He can accomplish His purposes in His strength through us.

This is when we begin to embark upon living the purpose God created us for.

---

[7] Colossians 3:15a

SPIRITUAL GIFTS

Every believer has been given at least one spiritual gift, and usually more than one. If you do not know what your spiritual gifts are, pray and ask the Holy Spirit to reveal them to you. Inquire at your church about taking a class on spiritual gifts or a spiritual gifts test. These tests often help people understand themselves and give them encouragement to begin operating in their gifts.

4. What are you naturally good at? What are your gifts and your talents? What are your passions?

   _____

   _____

5. According to Romans 12:4-8, what are some of the gifts and talents that God gives to believers?

   _____

   _____

We bring attention to God when we use our talents and abilities to cause others to want to know Him personally. We use our abilities and our talents for God's glory when we use them in such a way that others are drawn to want to know our Jesus.

What are your gifts? Do you like to teach? Are you good at prophecy? Are you an encourager? Are you a generous giver? Are you a leader? Are you good at administrative tasks? Do you have a gift of hospitality?

What are your passions? Do you have a passion for those who are homeless? For the poor? For unborn children? For Africa or any other foreign land? For politics? For putting a stop to human trafficking? For youth? For children? For women? For writing? For the mentally ill? For building homes with organizations like Habitat for Humanity? Do you have the joyful compulsion to pray for others, as an intercessor?

What is your profession? Are you a nurse? A doctor? An engineer? An accountant? A homemaker? An artist? Are you good at business? Do you like to sing? Are you an athlete? A designer? A writer? Are you technically savvy? Are you a chef?

What about your hobbies? Hiking? Running? Playing sports? Playing bridge? Cooking? Taking care of children? Reading? Painting?

We all want to make a difference in this world and in the lives of others. Yet all too often, we minimize the impact the Lord desires us to have NOW with what He's already given us. Use your gifts to impact your corner of the world by allowing God to take and anoint the things you may consider to be mundane or common. When surrendered to His Mighty hands, our lives will have significance, purpose, influence and we will be fruitful.

My accountant, Dina, is a wife and homeschooling mother of 4 children. She also happens to be a licensed CPA. Dina has very little extra time for activities outside of her family, so she has learned she can only do a few things with excellence.

Yet Dina is the reason that *Knowing God Ministries* exists as a 501(c)3. Dina has extensive knowledge about forming nonprofit organizations. She used that knowledge and passion to push and to guide me through the complicated path of creating a nonprofit entity. She continues to offer her gifts and time to the ministry by handling all our financials. She serves on my Board of Directors and makes herself available to me for counsel and wisdom. Not only that, but she is faithful to pray, and to cook for families in crisis. And as a side note, Dina and her husband, Brad both freely give of their time and talents to *Knowing God Ministries* as a couple. Where it not for his encouragement, she would simply not be available.

6. Are you using your gifts, talents, passions and abilities to bring attention to Jesus? If so, how?

_____

7. If not, has God dropped any ideas or opened doors of opportunity as to how could you take your gifts, passions and hobbies, and use them in a way to bring attention to Jesus?

_____

If you are unsure as to how to answer this question, it's okay. But spend time with God, allowing Him to share His passions and His concerns for the world around you. He'll give you a passion for the things that are on His heart. And when He does, be looking at the opportunities He may bring across your path, and then proceed prayerfully.

TAKING THE JESUS THING TOO FAR

When I sense people implying that, I'm taking this whole religion or Jesus thing *"just a bit too far,"* as we say in the south, I know this is a trick of the enemy, and I don't fall for it anymore. I quickly remind myself, "Where were these people when I was lying prostrate on the floor of my office in tears because following hard after God required every ounce of faith I could muster? Where were these people when my heart was so broken that no human words could make it better?

I can tell you where my Jesus was.

He was on the floor with me, placing His Word in my heart as the Holy Spirit was reminding me of Scriptures that I know or had studied. He'd bring passages to mind that consoled me, counseled me, and comforted me. He gave me words that were so perfect; words that were so relevant and hopeful that I knew that the power and presence of God was in room with me. It was almost tangible!

This has not just happened once or twice, but time and time again when my heart aches in such a way that there are no human words that can bring comfort, but only the Words of God Himself. Something happens in your heart when you experience Him to this degree. There's no going back. Going back would be like turning on your friend who helped you in your darkest hour.

So when someone implies, *"You're taking this Jesus stuff a little too far,"* do not be moved. Your Jesus will be there with you in such a way that it's impossible for you to be the same.

JOURNAL RESPONSE

Take a few moments to meditate on our study today.

Were there particular Scripture(s) or statement(s) that spoke to you personally?

1.

2.

3.

TODAY'S TREASURE

...

"I WILL REPAY YOU FOR THE YEARS
THE LOCUSTS HAVE EATEN."
JOEL 2:25

DREAM AGAIN

One cold, rainy, dreary afternoon in February 2004, I asked God in utter desperation, *"Is this all there is to life? Is this as good as it gets?"* It was the umpteenth diaper change and I was weary.

My children were 1 and 3, and it had been my life-long dream to become a stay-at-home mom. Now, by God's grace and the willingness of my husband, I was a stay-at-home-mom! My dreams had become realized! In fact, as a child, I had dreamed about being a stay-at-home mom. I used to pretend to be a mom and wife when I played with childhood friends. Now that was a reality, yet something was wrong. Why was I so discontent? I had everything a woman my age could possibly want: a great man, two healthy children, a beautiful house in one of my city's premier locations, and plenty of food in the pantry. I think I even had someone cleaning my house at the time. What was wrong with me? Why was I so discontent? What was this something that seemed to be missing? I felt so guilty for even feeling this way.

Little did I know then that God was redirecting my dreams. He was making room in my heart for HIS DREAMS.

At the time, I was in the process of becoming a Jesus Girl. During my children's nap-time, I'd say, *"NO"* to rest of the world and sit at Jesus' feet, reading His Word and trying to figure out how it applied to my everyday life. Suddenly, the day after I had asked God in such desperation if what I had was all there was, 1 Timothy 4:12-16 jumped off the page and into my heart. God seemed to be speaking directly to me.

"No, Tara, it isn't." He seemed to tell me.
In fact, *don't let anyone look down on you because you are young, but set an example for believers in speech, in life, in love, in faith and in purity. Until I come, devote yourself to the public reading of Scripture, to preaching and to teaching. Do not neglect your gift… Be diligent in these matters; give yourself wholly to them, so that everyone may see your progress. Watch your life and your doctrine closely. Persevere in them, because if you do, you will save both yourself and your hearers."*

I cannot articulate it any clearer than to simply say that something inside of me knew, one day, I'd have a speaking ministry. At that time, nothing was happening in my life that would give any credence to what I sensed God saying. I wasn't doing any speaking at all. No one, not even my husband, knew that I had a secret passion and a desire to one day teach God's Word. I had never shared that with anyone for fear that they would laugh or discourage me. But God knew, and He would one day take this passion and use it for His purposes. At the time, motherhood was His purpose for me (and still is!). But one day, He would be adding to this purpose.

In 2005, I moved closer to having a speaking ministry as God transitioned me from facilitating women in Bible study to teaching 4-year-olds God's Word! I instinctively knew that this was a training ground for greater service in God's kingdom. Most people saw it as a demotion. I saw it as a promotion, because now I could actually teach God's Word, whereas before, I could only facilitate small group study questions. (Do you see the importance of being a good steward wherever God places you?)

It would be June 2007 before I received my first speaking invitation.

1. **What do you dream about? You don't have to share if you'd rather not.**

   _____

   _____

2. **Do you have dreams that no one but God knows about?**

   _____

   _____

BROKEN DREAMS

Were you able to answer the above questions? Do you even dream anymore? For some of us, dreaming is a thing of the past and a waste of time because it's so far from the reality that we currently live. For others of us, we have experienced such broken or shattered dreams that we're scared to dream for fear of being disappointed yet again.

3. **How can Joel 2:25 bring encouragement and hope to the places in your dreams long devastated?**

   _____

Our God is a Redeemer. He is a Healer and He is ABLE, dear sister, to bring restoration to the ruins of our heart and hope to the places long devastated by illness, divorce, job loss, miscarriage, wayward teenagers, abandonment, abuse, or drinking addictions… He is able to restore the years the locusts have eaten.

DISCONTENT AND UNFULFILLED

Or the flip side of broken dreams: We are discontent when we've accomplished every personal goal and have received all of life's accolades. Dear sister, apart from God, every single human being will still have a feeling of emptiness if we are experiencing all life has to offer apart from relationship with Jesus. Do not be fooled! No relationship, no substance, no form of entertainment, no vacation, no job, no amount of food, beverage or drug can fill the void that is meant for a meaningful relationship with God. He is the One who fills the empty places in our life and will give us His dreams for our life… If we are willing to receive them.

When we feel empty, dissatisfied and discontent even when we seem to have all that this world has to offer, there's a reason. So instead of buying more or consuming more or eating more or inhaling more or working more, connect with the God of the Universe who made us, who has dreams and plans for us that will bring fulfillment and joy unlike anything else this world can offer. He'll place in our heart His dreams and His purposes for our life, if we are willing to receive them.

WEEK 7 | DAY 3

4. Have you ever experienced discontentment when your dreams have been realized? If so, share.

   _____
   _____

5. Are you willing to ask God to give you His dreams for your life? _____

6. If so, would you write a prayer to God now, in the space below? You can be as brief as you'd like or you can pour out your heart to Him. Tell Him if you're disappointed in how things in your life have turned out, if this is the case. Ask Him to redeem your life and bring restoration to the places long devastated by a past lifestyle or by things done to you. Or if you've experienced it all and you still sense that something is missing, surrender your dreams and ask Him to give you HIS perfect dreams for your life.

   _____
   _____
   _____
   _____
   _____

If you are alive and breathing, you have a purpose. You were not meant to live a mundane, mediocre life where you just muddle through the day. If this is the cycle you currently find yourself in – STOP! Start spending quality time with Jesus on a regular basis. Listen for His words of direction, His healing, His encouragement and comfort.

STICK YOUR FOOT IN THE WATER

Read Joshua 3:9-17

7. What did the Ark of the Covenant represent? _____

8. What went ahead of the people? (v14) _____

The ark of the covenant represented the Presence of God. Take note that the priests who were called to carry the ark went ahead of the people. I don't want you to miss this, sweet sister: whatever God may be calling us to, His Presence always goes ahead of us and makes a way. He makes a way even when our circumstances scream, *"There is NO way."*

9. What do you notice about the circumstances associated with the crossing of the Jordan? (v15)

   _____

If there was ever a time that it seemed impossible to the naked eye to cross the Jordan, it was at that moment when the river was at flood stage. So it is with our lives. It has been my experience that God will often call us to do something that seems impossible. Yet He's shown us in His Word, He's given us peace in our hearts, He's even allowed the godly women in our lives to confirm His direction in our lives, all when our circumstances look to us like *"flood stage."*

10. What did the priests do? _____

11. What did it require? _____

If you are convinced that God has willed the action, go the extra faith mile and believe that God will handle the circumstances. The priests had to stick their feet in the water. They had to place all their faith in the Lord God Almighty. They couldn't look at their circumstances, or the opinions of others, or depend on their resources, or even trust their feelings. They had to take a step of obedience by putting their feet in the water.

12. **The moment they placed their feet in the water, what did God do? (v16)**

_____

In 2011, when the *Knowing God Ministries* team and I set out to find a location for our luncheon, all doors seemed shut, especially the one we wanted opened most: a private country club that had convenient highway access for anyone in the state who wanted to come. This private country club also helped us keep our event from being labeled a denominational function – because women often resist attending if the function is not a part of their denomination. And I wanted my team serving the spiritual food, not the physical food. This private country club seemed to be a perfect fit. Yet our circumstances screamed, *"Give up! Impossible!"* I even began to question the call to begin these lunches. Yet our team persevered in prayer anyway.

One day, we decided to put our feet in the water by making an appointment with the Food and Beverage Manager and having lunch at the location we sensed God directing us to. As we had lunch that day, we prayed as we sat at the table, asking God to give us *"this land"* if it was His will and desire. After lunch, we met with the F&B manager. The cost to rent the room was so far from what we could afford that the circumstances seemed impossible.

The next morning in my quiet time, the Lord spoke to me out of Joshua. *"Now Jericho was tightly shut."* I thought, well, the country club where we want to have Your lunch is tightly shut.

The next verse: *"See, I have delivered Jericho into your hands."* God might as well have said, *"Tara, I have delivered this private country club into your hands,"* because later that same day, I received an email from the F&B Manager lowering the room rate to a rate that the ministry could afford! We just had to be willing to sign a one year contract![8]

This was the God of the Universe delivering Jericho into our hands, pushing back the waters of impossibility because one woman and her team obediently stuck their feet in the water despite the fact that it was at flood stage.

When God says move, MOVE! Put your foot in the water! The consequences of our obedience are His problem, not ours! The good news is that we don't even have to be successful! Success in God's eyes is not measured by the results our world measures success by. Success in God's eyes is the degree of obedience to His Word. Wholehearted obedience is success in God's eyes!

If we've been obedient to what God has told us to do, we have to trust the consequences of our obedience to Him.

---

8   At this writing, we just celebrated our 2 year anniversary!

WEEK 7 | DAY 3

JOURNAL RESPONSE

Take a few moments to meditate on our study today.

Were there particular Scripture(s) or statement(s) that spoke to you personally?

1.

2.

3.

WEEK 7 | DAY 4

TODAY'S TREASURE
...
"RUN IN SUCH A WAY AS TO GET THE PRIZE. EVERYONE WHO COMPETES IN THE GAMES GOES INTO STRICT TRAINING. THEY DO IT TO GET A CROWN THAT WILL NOT LAST; BUT WE DO IT TO GET A CROWN THAT WILL LAST FOREVER."
1 CORINTHIANS 9:24-25

Run so as to Win the Prize

The rubber is meeting the road, girlfriend. We're at the end of our study. I hope you've enjoyed our journey together as much as I have. Because of our study, I can't read the Bible anymore without seeing evidence throughout of the distinct purposes that God had for the people of bible times. Make no mistake, the God of the Bible is still the same God today, and He continues to have a purpose for every season of our lives.

However, as we close, I must be honest with you. My greatest fear is that you'll close the pages of this study, and you'll walk away perhaps STILL feeling that your life doesn't have purpose; that a life of purpose is only for the *special people*.

If this is you, let's just pretend I'm sitting across from you in a coffee shop. I have tears streaming down my face as I look at you intently eye-to-eye and share with you the value you have in the eyes of our God. He loves you completely and fully despite what your past or your present looks like. He wants you to know that He made you special, and that He's calling you to walk with Him each and every day for the rest of your life. If you'll only say "yes" to Him, He will give your life such meaning and value as He takes you on the adventure of a lifetime that we call life. Take the passages of Scripture we've studied and ask the Holy Spirit to make them "bone of your bone, flesh of your flesh" until they become living reality in your everyday life.

Know with great certainty that you were created for a purpose. And not just any purpose, but a God-ordained plan that was mapped out especially for you by your Creator. I don't want you to miss out on all God has planned for you. And selfishly, for the Body of Christ, think of what this world would look like, if the Body of Christ were functioning as God intended with His people walking in daily obedience ?! Our world would be an entirely different place. If you are alive and breathing – you have purpose on this planet!

1. **I want you to answer honestly. Do you believe that you have a purpose in life? That you were born for a reason? Or do you believe that we are all here by accident? Or by the whim of some cosmic event?**

CREATED FOR PURPOSE

2. Over the course of the last few weeks, what are some of the things the Lord has revealed that you don't want to forget?

_____

_____

3. Over the course of the last few weeks, what are some of the things the Lord has spoken into your heart with respect to your purpose for this season in life?

_____

_____

THE KEYS TO YOUR LIFE

John 15:7-11

4. What makes the Father most happy? In other words, what glorifies the Father? (v8)

_____

5. What is the prerequisite for fruit-bearing? (v9-10) _____

_____

6. What is the prerequisite for a life of such joy that Jesus describes it as, *"that your joy may be complete."* (v10-11)

_____

Do you see? We weren't created to be just a little fruitful – we were created for MUCH FRUIT-BEARING. It's in the fruit bearing that we begin to experience and live in joy that is so great that Jesus describes it as *"joy complete."* This is the key to finding abundant life! But understand, our fruitfulness is completely dependent on our attachment to the Vine, Jesus. We can't live beside the Vine and expect to live fruitful, purposeful lives. In other words, an hour on Sunday morning won't cut it! We have to live attached to the Vine, grafted onto Him.

One of the things that I love about the Bible is how God weaves the same thread throughout the entire canon of Scripture. Let's look at this Old Testament verse and compare its similarities to John 15.

Deuteronomy 30:19-20 NTL (Bold mine)

> *"Today I have given you the choice between life and death, between blessings and curses. Now I call on heaven and earth to witness the choice you make.* ***Oh, that you would choose life****, so that you and your descendants may live!* ***You can make this choice by loving the Lord your God, obeying Him, and committing yourself firmly to Him. This is the key to your life.*** *And if you love and obey the Lord, you will live long in the land the Lord swore to give your ancestors Abraham, Isaac, and Jacob."*

7. What is the key to life?

8. What similarities do you notice between Deuteronomy and John?

From cover to cover, loving the Lord your God with all you heart, mind and soul requires knowing Him, not just knowing about Him, and involves spending time with Him – quality time – on a regular basis. Loving Him also means choosing obedience rather than disobedience. There, my friend, you have the keys to abundant life!

KEYS TO PURPOSE

I so want you to get this. Not only get it, but live it! So let me sum it up so that you can easily memorize it or refer back to it.

The key to your life:

> **A. Having a relationship with the God of the Universe through Jesus Christ.**
>
> **B. Spending time cultivating this relationship.**
>
> **C. Spending time listening to Him.**
>
> **D. Obeying AND persevering in what we believe He has said.**

RUN WITH PURPOSE

9. **From Today's Treasure in 1 Corinthians 9:24, how are we to live our lives?**

Did you catch the phrase, *"in such a way"*? It means In such a way that you are not brainwashed by what the culture tells you will bring value and purpose to your life, In such a way that when you stand before God – and you will – that you will not be ashamed. That you will have no regrets, because you ran in such a way that you are noticeably **different** from the world around you because you're "plugged into" the Holy Spirit each day, obeying and following His directives for every situation and for every season of your life.

10. **What is the *prize*? Your answer will be found in Week 2. (Hint: gold...)**

11. **How does the crown that will not last remind you of Brainwashed Boulevard and the wood, the hay, and the straw?**

12. How can we keep from living aimlessly day after day? (You know the answer – it's all we've talked about!)

_____

We live with the end in mind by living a life that is focused on Jesus each day, allowing Him to vicariously live through us using our talents and abilities wherever He has strategically placed us on planet Earth. The prize: one day when we stand before Him, we will not be ashamed. We will have no regrets because we will be able to place at His feet gold, silver, and the costly stones of changed lives and changed hearts in our generation because we determined to be *"Jesus girls,"* to not live life as usual, but to love, obey and serve Him with focused perseverance.

FINAL WORDS

The life God has called me to, I never would have chosen for myself. John 15:16 says, *"You did not choose Me, but I chose you and appointed you to go and bear fruit – fruit that will last."* But, I would not change anything in my life. Why? Because I have

- A **joy** that's indescribable.
- A **peace** that nothing else can give from living in the center of God's will.
- A **quiet confidence** that comes from trusting and relying upon God to open doors of opportunity and to provide for every need.

Your purpose and my purpose will not be the same, but we all have a God-ordained purpose. You cannot live someone else's purpose, and you cannot compare your purpose to another person's. Just as our individual fingerprints are unique, so will be our God-ordained purpose in each season of life also be unique.

So if you are not already, start living the "Jesus girl" lifestyle. Like the early disciples, allow Jesus to work through you in such a way that you turn your corner of the world upside down much like Jesus' uneducated, unschooled band of brothers did in the early church. Their actions ***forever changed the world.*** Their obedience in their generation is the reason you and I know Jesus today and can have a life purpose. Talk about impacting the generations! Lest Jesus tarry in returning, may the same be said of us by our descendants, *"That because of my mother; because of my grandmother or because my great grandmother knew and loved Jesus, my family is different today because we know, love and serve the Living God of the Universe."*

Quite possibly, you too would not choose what God has chosen for you and for your family. But whatever it is, it will bring joy that is so complete that your soul will hunger for nothing more than knowing and doing His will in your everyday life. So don't run from what God may be calling you to… Or you may be missing out on the adventure of a lifetime!

REVIEW

1. What were the most meaningful or significant lessons you learned each day?

   Day 1: _____

   _____

   Day 2: _____

   _____

   Day 3: _____

   _____

   Day 4: _____

   _____

2. Is there anything you sense God telling you to do as a result of the study this week? If so, share.

   _____

   _____

3. What action steps do you need to take in order to be obedient?

   _____

   _____

CREATED FOR PURPOSE